A Guide to the Common Core Writing Workshop

Intermediate Grades

Lucy Calkins

Photographs by Peter Cunningham

HEINEMANN ◆ PORTSMOUTH, NH

DEDICATED TO TEACHERS™

*first*hand
An imprint of Heinemann
361 Hanover Street
Portsmouth, NH 03801–3912
www.heinemann.com

Offices and agents throughout the world

The author and publisher wish to thank those who have generously given permission to reprint borrowed material:

ISBN-13: 978-0-325-04799-7
ISBN-10: 0-325-04799-5

Production: Elizabeth Valway, David Stirling, and Abigail Heim
Cover and interior designs: Jenny Jensen Greenleaf
Series includes photographs by Peter Cunningham, Nadine Baldasare, and Elizabeth Dunford
Composition: Publishers' Design and Production Services, Inc.
Manufacturing: Steve Bernier

Printed in the United States of America on acid-free paper

17 16 15 14 13   ML   1 2 3 4 5

Contents

Acknowledgments

THIS SERIES IS THE BIGGEST UNDERTAKING of my life—other than the larger projects of leading the Teachers College Reading and Writing Project and of parenting Miles and Evan—and so it is fitting that I dedicate this project to my mother and my father. I thank Evan and Virginia Calkins for all that I am, for all that I believe in, and for giving me eight brothers and sisters—Sally, Steve, Joan, Ben, Hugh, Ellen, Geoff, and Tim—and thirty-some nieces and nephews. Two of the many young people in the extended clan are my sons, Miles and Evan Skorpen. Anyone who has ever read my writing or been part of my teaching knows that the sun rises and sets for me with Miles and Evan. Those of you who have followed their writing through all the years may miss the new infusions of their drafts; they have both become young men now, and I'm not chronicling their comings and goings in quite the same way. John and I could not be more proud of them.

I live and learn as part of the community of teacher-educators that comprises the Teachers College Reading and Writing Project, and all of the people at the Project are my thought-companions. I especially thank Laurie Pessah and Kathleen Tolan, senior deputy directors; Mary Ehrenworth, deputy director for middle school and coauthor of *Pathways to the Common Core*; and Amanda Hartman, associate director. These people are my closest friends, my life partners, and I can't imagine any more beautiful way to work and live than alongside them. I also thank Mary Ann Mustac and the team of fifty-plus full-time staff developers who keep the Project's work vital, robust, and grounded. These people, too, are my partners.

At the desk, my closest partner is Kate Montgomery. Kate and I have imagined, planned, written, and revised all the Units of Study series, since their origin. I was only willing to undertake this gigantic all-new CCSS-aligned effort after Kate agreed to work half-time as essentially the senior coauthor of the entire series. Kate's brilliant mind is ever-present in all of these books and in the design of the entire effort.

The ideas about teaching writing that are essential in this book have been evolving since I was a young teacher. Starting then and continuing for years afterward, I worked very closely with two people who opened the field of writing to me and to the world. Other than my parents, Don Graves and Don Murray changed my life more than anyone else. My pathway would have been entirely different had these two incredible mentors not shown me a terrain to explore, given me tools with which to do that exploring, and most of all, empowered me to rise to the occasion.

Words can't easily contain my gratitude to all the coauthors who joined me in writing these books. I thank each individually within the particular books, but some have helped with books beyond their own. Amanda Hartman's knowledge of young children has been like a bottomless well from which many of us drink continually. Julia Mooney's impeccable standards and her deep knowledge make her a pillar of strength. Kathleen Tolan's originality and her fearless focus on excellence makes her a never-ending source of insight. In a ten-minute conversation, Mary Ehrenworth can illuminate any conundrum, helping me see a path. She has also helped me care deeply about the Common Core State Standards. Ali Marron's writing skill and enormous heart have made her the perfect person to have close by during writing work. Kelly Boland Hohne's searing intelligence has left many of us feeling breathless—and blessed. Janet Steinberg's hand on the pulse of teacher effectiveness, curricular mapping, Depth of Knowledge (DOK), and the CCSS has kept us all hopping. Audra Robb has made us smarter in the arena of performance assessments. The infusion of fresh potent teaching from Hareem Khan, often working by candlelight due to power failures in remote corners of

Pakistan, has kept us going. Many school principals have opened their doors to us—none more often than Adele Schroder, PS 59; Melanie Woods, PS 29; Anthony Inzerillo, 199 Queens; Katy Rosen, 199 Manhattan; Daryl Adalhoff, PS 158, and Cheryl Tyler 277, Bronx. Peter Cunningham, the photographer for every book I've ever written, graced this effort with magical talent.

Teva Blair and Abby Heim worked together with Kate Montgomery to lead Heinemann's involvement with this effort, and I thank them both for channeling enormous support toward this project. Teva Blair has kept her hand on the pulse of the entire enterprise, managing the people, the texts, and the dates, and, above all, bringing a knack for structure and knowledge of the project to her marvelous editing efforts. Abby Heim has been the production mastermind at Heinemann. She has kept track of all the zillions of bits and pieces that create the mosaic of these books, and done so with a combination of strength, resolve, and focus that keeps everyone's attention on the job at hand. She's also been the emotional leader of the enterprise, bringing maturity and experience to that role. This team works under the direction of Lesa Scott, who is at the helm of Heinemann, and I thank her for recognizing the significance of this effort and devoting resources and talent to it. Charles McQuillen and Buzz Rhodes will take over once Abby and Teva let go, and I thank them in advance for what they will do to usher the books into the hands of teachers.

Most of all, I am grateful to Kate Montgomery, who is my writing partner and co-leader of this entire effort. Kate and I imagined the series together, made the hard decisions together, devised the principles and structures that unify the series together, and supported the coauthors together. It has been a great joy to share responsibility for authoring the ideas and the books in the series with Kate. Her writing embodies the crystal clarity and the warmth that E. B. White describes in his *Elements of Style*. Her knowledge of teaching and literacy research has grown from a lifetime of work with many of the best thinkers in the field. How blessed this project has been to have her constant and close involvement.

A Note to My Readers

IN A MOMENT, I'm going to ask that you step with me into this series, into this world of writing plans and teaching strategies and exciting new ideas for fostering developmental breakthroughs in children. In some ways I think of this project as the culmination of my life work so far; it grows from decades of think tanks and teaching and coaching and studying with my colleagues and with teachers from around the world. It represents not only my best work but also the best work of more than thirty of my colleagues. Here, then, is the grand unveiling of this master work, and I am so eager to share it with you!

Nonetheless, I want to ask you to stop for a moment before you read on. Before you turn to the ins and outs of curriculum and the face of education today, the new standards and old standards and best practices, pause for a moment to picture the face of a child. One small someone you know well. When you see her running up to you, does it make you smile? When you picture him, walking slowly away with his head down, backpack slumped over his shoulder, do you want to reach out, maybe call him back? And when you think of all of them, their quirky, tousled, grubby, beautiful faces looking up at you expectantly, I know you feel the tug in your chest, that tug of feeling we are so responsible for them all. We feel it deeply. And this is what I want to say: *that* is the core of all that matters in teaching. Without that care, the greatest curriculum in the world is only paper and a little dry ink.

Chapter 1

A New Mission for Schools and Educators

"The new mission . . . is to get all students to meet high standards of education and to provide them with a lifelong education that does not have built-in obsolescence of so much old-style curriculum but that equips them to be lifelong learners."

—Michael Fullan, Peter Hill, and Carmel Crévola, *Breakthrough*

IN A WORLD that is increasingly dominated by big corporations and big money, it is easy for individuals to feel silenced. No one is more apt to be silenced than children, who too often grow up being taught to be obedient rather than to be wise, empathetic, and critical. The teaching of writing can change that. In a democracy, we must help young people grow up to know how to voice their ideas, know how to speak out for what is right and good.

The information age of today makes it especially imperative that young people, not just an elite few but all students, develop skills that are significantly more complex than those required of them in the past. In part, the increased focus on writing comes from the technological revolution that has transformed our lives. As the ways of communicating— text messaging, email, social media, search engines—seep into every nook and cranny of our day, all of us are writing more than ever. Today, it has become increasingly important for all children to be given an education that enables them to synthesize, organize, reflect on, and respond to the data in their world. Indeed, several years ago, the National Commission on Writing called for a "Writing Revolution," suggesting that children needed to double the amount of time they spent writing in their classrooms. Students need to be able to write not only narratives but also to write arguments and information texts. They need not only to record information and ideas but also to synthesize, analyze, compare, and contrast that information and those ideas.

In their important book, *Breakthrough* (2006), Michael Fullan, Peter Hill, and Carmel Crévola point out that the old mission for schools used to be to provide universal access to basic education and then to provide a small, choice group entry to a university education. Although that mission may have made sense in the world of our parents, it no longer makes sense. Whereas twenty years ago 95% of jobs were low skilled, today those jobs only constitute 10% of our entire economy (Darling-Hammond et al., *Powerful Learning: What We Know about Teaching for Understanding*, 2008). Children who leave school today without strong literacy skills will no longer find a job waiting for them. "The new mission . . . is to get *all* students to meet high standards of education and to provide them with a lifelong education that does not have built-in obsolescence of so much old-style curriculum but that equips them to be lifelong learners." These words are from the prelude to *Breakthrough*, but they could also appear in the prelude to the Common Core State Standards or the prelude to this book.

As this nation wakes up to the fact that the education millions of Americans received in the past simply isn't adequate for today, more and more schools are realizing that one of the most potent ways to accelerate students' progress as learners is by equipping them with first-rate skills in writing. While the teaching of writing had no place in the NCLB standards of yesteryear, there has been an about-face since then, and the Common Core State Standards give equal attention to writing as they do to reading—and even suggest that students' abilities to read will be assessed through their abilities to write.

For teachers, parents, and students in schools that have not taught writing in the past, the exemplar student writing showcased in Appendix B of the Common Core (and the standards themselves that detail what all students are now expected to know and be able to do) may feel like pie in the sky. I've seen teachers guffaw at some of the samples of student writing included in the Common Core as if that work represents an utterly inaccessible goal. That's not a surprising response from educators who have not, themselves, received help teaching writing. What we now know about writing development is that students need extensive opportunities to write on topics they care about, they need explicit and sequenced instruction that helps them develop along a learning progression, and they need critical feedback that helps them know next steps. It's a tall order for teachers to provide those conditions to students if they themselves have only received minimal instruction in writing and/or have not taken a single course in the teaching of writing.

But the good news is that the student samples in the appendix are representative of what many students have been doing for a long time. Educators need not feel empty-handed when they ask, "How can we begin to approach the challenge of meeting Common Core expectations in writing?" Instead, there are schools across the country that have traveled a good portion of that journey and can help other schools get started. Although many school leaders are just now waking up to the importance of teaching writing, many of us across the nation have had those concerns at heart for a long time. At the Teachers College Reading and Writing Project, for example, we have been working for three decades to develop, pilot, revise, and implement state-of-the-art curriculum in teaching writing. We have had a chance to do this work under the influence of the Common Core for the past few years, and this series—this treasure chest of experiences, theories, techniques, tried-and-true methods, and questions—will bring the results of that work to you.

THE WRITING WORKSHOP: GROWTH FOR STUDENTS *AND* TEACHERS

Word has spread. The hundreds of thousands of teachers who used an earlier, very different edition of this series have spread the word that the writing workshop has given their children unbelievable power not only as writers but also as thinkers, learners, and readers. School districts are finding that when teachers receive the education they deserve in the teaching of writing, those teachers are able to provide students with clear, sequenced, vibrant writing instruction (along with opportunities to write daily for their own important purposes), and this makes a dramatic difference in young people's abilities to write. Powerful writing instruction produces visible and immediate results; the stories, petitions, speeches, and essays that students produce become far more substantial and significant, revealing the young authors' ideas in ways that make parents, community members, and the children themselves sit up and take notice.

When young people are explicitly taught the craft of proficient writing, they are able to travel the world as writers, applying their skills to discipline-based learning and to their lives. And through all of this work, their writing skills continue to develop. When I work with teachers, I often say to them, "If your students' writing skills are not visibly, dramatically improving after a few weeks of instruction, you are doing something wrong." Over all these years, it has become crystal clear to us that when teaching writing, good teaching pays off. When you provide students with constant opportunities to write and when you actively and assertively teach into their best efforts, their development as writers will astonish you, their parents, the school administrators, and best of all, the youngsters themselves.

It is not only *children's* work that is transformed when teachers are supported in the teaching of writing; *teachers'* work is also transformed. One of the beautiful things about teaching writing is that no one needs to make a choice between responsive, developmentally appropriate teaching and results-oriented, data-based teaching. The good news is that when children write, their thinking, their progress, their vulnerabilities will inevitably be right there before your eyes—and before their eyes, too. Whereas reading must be translated into something that is no longer reading for it to be assessed, in black and white, growth in writing is always concrete, demonstrable, and evidenced based.

Then, too, when a community of teachers embraces reform in the teaching of writing, teachers often become reinvigorated and renewed in the process. And individual teachers find that teaching writing taps new sources of energy within themselves. Over the years, teachers have repeatedly told me that the teaching of writing has given them new energy, clarity, and compassion, reminding them why they went into teaching in the first place. I understand what these teachers mean, for writing has done all this—and more—for me as well.

All of this creates an escalating demand for professional development in writing.

THE SERIES: BOTH CURRICULUM *AND* PROFESSIONAL DEVELOPMENT

The Units of Study series has been written in ways that double as both curricular support and professional development. Each day's instruction is designed according to research-based principles. For example, you will see that in one day after another, all of the teaching follows the "gradual release

of responsibility" model of teaching. Students can first learn from a demonstration (accompanied by an explicit explanation), then from guided practice in which the amount of scaffolding they receive lessens over time, and then from independent work, for which they receive feedback. Then, too, you'll see that when we first use a new method, it is simplified and streamlined. We take the time to coach students so they understand their role in that process. Over time, the method becomes more layered and complex, fluid and implicit.

The progressions that you will see in our teaching are always carefully chosen and explicitly explained. Our goal is to highlight the replicable teaching moves in ways that allow you to transfer those same moves to curriculum that you invent. I know from helping thousands of teachers learn to teach writing that these units will scaffold and inform your own teaching, and you will develop and finesse with flexibility the methods and information conveyed in these books.

"One of the most potent ways to accelerate students' progress as learners is by equipping them with first-rate skills in writing."

The wonderful thing about learning to teach writing well is that there are just a few teaching methods that one needs to know and be able to use. In this series, I provide crystal-clear advice on how to lead efficient and effective minilessons, conferences, and small-group strategy sessions. I do so knowing that as you travel through the series, encountering scores of transcripts of minilessons, conferences, small-group sessions, and shares, you will learn not only from explicit instruction but also from immersion. This—the first book of the series—explicitly describes the architecture of all our minilessons, conferences, and small-group strategy sessions and details the management techniques that make writing workshops possible. *Writing Pathways: Performance Assessments and Learning Progressions, K–5* provides you with an assessment system that can make teaching and learning robust, goal directed, data based, and responsive. The unit books show these methods and principles affecting real-life classrooms.

Ideally, you and every other teacher in the world should be able not only to observe exemplary teaching but also to do so with a coach nearby, highlighting the way the teaching illustrates a collection of guiding principles. Therefore, as you witness my teaching and that of my colleagues, I will also be an ever-present coach, underscoring aspects of the teaching that seem especially essential. My goal is to enable you to extrapolate guidelines and methods as you watch this teaching, so that on another day you'll begin to invent your own teaching. After all, these books provide a detailed model; they are not meant as a script. The end goal is not the teaching that we've described here but the teaching that you, your colleagues, and your children invent together.

AN OVERVIEW OF THE SERIES

This one book—*A Guide to the Common Core Writing Workshop*—accompanies the series of books written for third-grade teachers, for fourth-grade teachers, and also for fifth-grade teachers. (I've also written a similar guide for kindergarten, first-, and second-grade teachers.) Each grade's series contains:

- The *Guide to the Common Core Writing Workshop*
- Four Common Core–aligned units of study, including one unit each in opinion, information, and narrative writing
- A book of alternate and additional units, *If . . . Then . . . Curriculum*, written to help you differentiate curriculum
- *Writing Pathways: Performance Assessments and Learning Progressions, K–5*, a book that puts a system for assessing writing into your hands and into the hands of your students
- A CD-ROM, *Resources for Teaching Writing*, of additional resources, including sample student writing, reproducible checklists, and Web links

The intent of this series is to support students' abilities to be strategic, metacognitive writers who use particular processes to achieve particular purposes as writers. Within a grade and across grades, the books fit tongue-and-groove alongside each other. Together, they help students consolidate and use what they have learned so that they meet and exceed the Common Core State Standards for each grade. More importantly, the books help students learn to use writing as a tool for learning across the day and throughout their richly literate lives.

Four Common Core–Aligned Unit of Study Books

Each unit of study book represents about six weeks of teaching, and within those six weeks, the unit supports several cycles of drafting, revision, and publication. The units align with the three types of writing specified in the Common Core State Standards. For example, at each grade level, one or two of the unit of study books fall under the umbrella of opinion writing. In the third-grade unit, *Changing the World*, children write persuasive letters, petitions, and speeches. In fourth grade, there are two opinion units—one on the personal and persuasive essay and one on literary essays. In fifth grade, the culminating book of the series helps students tackle research-based argument essays. In the same way, there are units at each grade level that support students' development in narrative and information writing.

Then, at every grade, in addition to a book that supports each of the three types of writing highlighted in the CCSS, there is a fourth book. In third grade, this allows for a second narrative unit, this time on adapting fairy tales; in fourth grade, this allows for another book under the opinion umbrella—a book on writing essays about literature; in fifth grade, this allows for a memoir unit where some students elect to structure their writing as a narrative, and others, as an essay, letting the form follow meaning.

The books are written in a way that gives you the chance to listen in on and observe the unit being taught with students just the age of your students. It will seem as if you were invited into a classroom to watch and listen as my coauthors and I work with youngsters. You will listen as we convene the class into the meeting area for a ten-minute minilesson, channeling the children to sit beside partners, calling for their attention, and you'll hear how we talk about and demonstrate the strategies and skills of effective writing. Of course, you'll also overhear the jokes and stories we use to draw them in and the directions we give to send them off to their work time. Then, too, you'll hear the ways we confer and lead small groups to support the work they do during that day's workshop. You'll watch us teach writers to self-assess their writing early in a unit of study, becoming familiar with goals for that unit, and you'll see the way that learning progressions and data weave through every unit of study. You'll see pre- and postassessments bookend each unit of study.

Each of the four units of study books contains the words of our teaching (and students' responses to it) for that entire six-week-long unit of study. We also provide representative examples of the writing youngsters did in each unit of study.

Each Day in a Unit of Study Book

Once you begin teaching a unit, you will find that each day's teaching— each *session*—within that unit is introduced with a prelude that helps you to understand why, out of all that could possibly be taught at that juncture, we decided on that particular minilesson. The art of teaching comes from choice. The prelude, then, brings you in on the rationale behind the choices that inform the upcoming session. Why this minilesson? How will it fit with earlier and with later instruction? What are the real goals? The prelude highlights what matters most in the session, and hopefully it functions as a bit of a keynote speech, revving you up for the teaching that follows.

Then you can listen in to state-of-the-art *minilessons*, taught to children who are just the age of your class. Hear the language that I (and coauthors) use, and hear some of the ways children respond. Each minilesson follows the same structure, which is described in more detail in Chapter 7.

After we send students off to their work spots, my colleagues and I fill you in on the *conferring and small-group work* we are apt to do during the upcoming work time. More often than not, this section will be like a miniature workshop, showing you ways to teach responsively. That teaching will be punctuated with *mid-workshop teaching* that we give to the whole class, partway through writing time. Often this teaching builds on the minilesson, extending it by providing a next step or a follow-up point. Sometimes the mid-workshop teaching counterbalances the minilesson or broadcasts lessons being taught in conferences or small groups. Either way, most mid-workshop teachings are actually mini-minilessons! We also describe the whole-class share session that culminates the workshop.

By the time children are in the upper-elementary grades, they can do substantial work at home, and they will be more eager to do this work if you are careful to craft homework that helps children outgrow themselves. By fourth grade, most sessions contain suggested *homework* assignments. These are on the CD-ROM, as well as in the book, so that you can print them out for students to tape into their assignment pads.

A Book of Alternate and Additional Units

In addition to the four units of study for each grade level, we have written a grade-specific book, titled *If . . . Then . . . Curriculum: Assessment-Based Instruction*. Each of these books offers shortened versions of five to seven grade-specific units of study that you might decide to teach before, after, or in between the core curriculum. For example, if you worry that your fifth-graders didn't participate in the fourth-grade units on opinion writing—one

that introduces essay writing and one that supports literary essays—you'll wisely conclude that they don't have the background they need to take the unit *The Research-Based Argument Essay* by storm. In *If . . . Then . . . Curriculum: Assessment-Based Instruction*, you will receive practical help teaching a single essay unit that provides the most essential content from the units that your children missed. Similar help is given to support children who may not be ready for *The Lens of History: Research Reports*. Then again, your fifth-graders may instead be chomping at the bit for additional challenges, and the *If . . . Then . . . Curriculum* book provides you with detailed help teaching units in poetry, journalism, and fantasy. The curriculum we've described in great detail only supports half or two thirds of your school year so you will want to teach these additional units of study.

A Book of Assessment Tools

The curriculum set out in these units is integrated into an assessment system that includes three learning progressions, one in each type of writing, as well as grade-by-grade checklists, grade-specific rubrics, and three benchmark texts illustrating at-standards level, on-demand opinion, information, and narrative writing. An early version of this assessment system has been piloted in thousands of classrooms, and the entire system has been revised based on feedback.

Essentially, in this system, K–8 teachers begin the school year by asking students to spend forty-five minutes writing an on-demand narrative, and on other days, to spend similar time writing an on-demand information text and opinion text. In most schools, teachers decide that in each instance, students will merely be told to do their best writing. A teacher might say to her students, for example, "You have forty-five minutes to write your best personal narrative, Small Moment story, true story, or piece of short fiction—your best narrative. Write in a way that shows me all you know about narrative writing." Some schools prefer the prompt to be much more clearly delineated, with all the expectations spelled out, and we provide schools with both ways to word the tasks so you may choose the method you prefer.

Each student's work is then scored against a learning progression and an accompanying set of sample student texts in each genre that have been benchmarked to represent each level of the learning progression. For example, a reader can read the introduction in one child's information text, asking, "Does this match expectations for a third-grade introduction? A fourth-grade introduction? A fifth-grade one?" (There is also a way for teachers to score the piece as 2.5 or 3.5.) Then, teachers teach the students a unit on information writing, giving students ample opportunities to assess themselves at the beginning, middle, and end of the unit against checklists that spell out the goals they should be working toward. After the unit is completed, the on-demand assessment is repeated, and students' work is again scored. Presumably teachers will teach more than one unit in each of the three major kinds of writing, and the on-demands can be given periodically throughout the year to continue to track students' progress.

The most important thing about the learning progressions and performance assessments is that they enable teachers and students to grasp where students are in their writing development, so that you can figure out ways to help them move toward next steps. The assessment system that undergirds this curriculum is meant as an instructional tool. It makes progress in writing as transparent, concrete, and obtainable as possible and puts ownership for this progress into the hands of learners. As part of this, this system of assessment demystifies the Common Core State Standards, allowing students and teachers to work toward a very clear image of what good writing entails.

A CD-ROM of Additional Resources

The accompanying CD-ROM offers student samples, short video clips, Web links, and homework for grades 4 and 5. On the CD-ROM, you'll find reproducible checklists and rubrics, editing checklists, conferring scenarios (from the *If . . . Then . . . Curriculum* book) that can be printed on label paper so you can leave your students with an artifact of your teaching, and websites that will help you and your students do research for your writing projects. These resources will support your teaching throughout the year.

The Series Components All Together: A PreK–5 Learning Progression

If you are truly going to bring all of your students to the ambitious standards of the CCSS, there needs to be vertical alignment in the curriculum so that people who teach at any one grade level can count on students entering their classrooms with some foundational skills that can then be built on. The days of each teacher functioning as a Lone Ranger in the teaching of writing are at an end. Imagine how impractical it would be if each third-grade teacher decided whether to teach multiplication: fourth-grade teachers who received students from several different third grades would find that half the class had never learned anything but addition, and the other half would be chomping at the bit to study long division! Of course, almost every school *does* have a math curriculum that supports vertical alignment. Granted, even in a school where students are all taught multiplication in third grade, some students won't master those skills; still, there is agreement that a shared math curriculum means that teachers can extend and build on previous instruction. Until the release of the Common Core State Standards, many educators didn't realize that writing skills, too, need to be developed incrementally, with the work that students do at one grade level standing on the shoulders of prior learning.

In this series, instruction builds on itself. Often that instruction may have occurred in a different genre, within that same school year. For example, a teacher might say, "In your earlier unit of study in narrative writing, you learned that writers include the specific words that characters say. Today I want to teach you that including the exact words that people say is also important when writing a research report." In this way, you bring students to higher levels of achievement by making sure that your teaching stands on the shoulders of prior instruction.

Sometimes the prior instruction that undergirds a minilesson will have occurred during the previous year. "I know that last year, you learned that when writing about information, it helps to group your writing into sections. Last year, most of you grouped your writing into chapters, each addressing a different subtopic. This year, I want to tell you it is important to include a few sentences within your introductory paragraph that let readers know the plan for how you will group the information, for how those subsections will go."

Of course, teaching involves not only a well-planned curriculum but also deep assessment and responsive instruction. Students will be able to proceed up the vertical alignment in the series only if teachers use—and make teaching decisions based on—the assessments in this series. These assessments scaffold the curriculum and are also aligned both to the Common Core State Standards and with preceding grade levels' work. For example, the CCSS state that in fourth grade, writers must be able to orient readers at the start of a narrative. In the unit of study learning progressions, teachers can see ways to teach students to do this, and they can see how those techniques relate to what was taught in the preceding years. Using a rubric based on the learning progression for narrative writing, teachers can collect data that reveals which students still need help with that foundational skill, and they can alter their teaching accordingly.

WHAT'S CHANGED IN THIS NEW SERIES?

This series is not a second edition of the original Units of Study for Teaching Writing, Grades 3–5. It is a set of mostly (and sometimes entirely) new books.

The New Series Is Grade Specific

The biggest difference between this series and the former series is that the units of study are now grade specific. This means, for example, that the third-grade units of study take into account that many third-graders are writing on full sheets of notebook paper and in writer's notebooks for the first time. The opening unit, *Crafting True Stories*, serves not only to extend students' work with personal narrative but also as a launch into the very new expectations of third grade. In the third-grade book on information writing, youngsters write chapter books, learning to section their topics into subtopics. They are supported in this challenging work because they are writing about topics on which they have firsthand, personal knowledge: dogs, soccer, gymnastics. The third book for third graders, *Changing the World*, rallies youngsters to use their newfound abilities of gathering and organizing information, combined with their skills in persuasion, to persuade people about causes they believe matter: stopping bullying, recycling, saving the dogs at the SPCA. The final book in third grade invites children to adapt fairy tales, using familiar fairy tales as a scaffold within which they are taught techniques of fiction. The heady work of writing in scenes, linking scenes, and orienting readers through the use of an omniscient narrator, and using story structure to create tension and figurative language to convey mood is supported by the fact that children borrow from familiar fairy tales.

The fourth-grade series is written for children on the cusp of writing more academic texts. The meat-and-potatoes curriculum of the fourth-grade

series brings students into all the genres that will be especially essential from now through middle school. Students learn to write thesis-driven essays, including both persuasive and literary essays, and they learn to write research reports. They also learn to write realistic fiction and to see that the lenses they bring to reading fiction can also be brought to writing fiction. Although the fourth-grade year tackles the especially essential academic genre, each unit is absolutely steeped in a deep understanding of the youngsters. You'll see that the units begin where children are and give them a progression of instruction that brings them step by step toward increasing proficiency. For example, their earliest work in essay writing is a two-day boot camp that helps them write the simplest essays imaginable. Those early essays allow children to internalize the template of thesis, reasons, and evidence. The earliest essays are replaced with more complex ones, with students eventually writing the compare-and-contrast essays that are important to meeting CCSS expectations. In this way, the fourth-grade units all work together to provide a progression of skill development that has grown out of our work with hundreds of classrooms.

By the time children enter fifth grade, they will already have been introduced to most, if not all, of the new skills that are expected of fifth-graders. The sequence of the fifth-grade units consolidates those skills and then tackles most of the Common Core State Standards for sixth grade. Our experience has shown us that fifth grade can be an extraordinary year for writing development. Youngsters are chomping at the bit to do more, and fifth-grade teachers who work in self-contained classrooms, at least, have far better conditions for teaching writing than do their middle school compatriots. Experience has shown us that it's entirely possible for students to leave fifth grade having learned many of the skills called for in the sixth-grade standards: how to conduct research using primary sources, how to write narratives that are sequenced and theme based, and how to write argument essays that use counterargument to clarify a position.

Throughout the units, we've written not only with a specific grade level in mind but also with a specific time of year. After all, the difference between the beginning and the end of fourth grade can be just about as big as the difference between fifth grade and high school! The 3–5 units of study, then, are very different depending on if they are written for fall or for spring.

Because these units are written for specific grade levels, one unit is able to stand on the shoulders of the preceding unit. That is, the third-grade unit on fairy tales helps youngsters to recall and apply the knowledge they learned in the narrative unit at the start of the year. There are references to prior years' instruction, too, and we hope and expect that usually, these units will be taught as part of a coherent program of study. The *If . . . Then . . . Curriculum: Assessment-Based Instruction* book will help those of you whose children have not had prior instruction know how to alter your teaching accordingly.

The New Series Takes Up the Challenges of the CCSS for Writing and Exceeds Them

Of course, much of the impetus for this new series was the nation's widespread adoption of the Common Core State Standards. For those of us who know and love the writing workshop, it seems as if many aspects of the writing standards have been written with a writing workshop precisely in mind. The grade-by-grade standards fit our understanding of how young people develop within a writing workshop. To those of us who know the fingerprints of writing workshop instruction, it is clear that many of the exemplar texts in the appendix emerged from workshops.

However, the arrival of the CCSS has challenged even writing workshop advocates to develop more sequential, ambitious work in opinion/argument writing and in writing across the curriculum. We've responded to this wise challenge by developing a sequential, K–5 curriculum in opinion/argument and information writing and by giving renewed attention to particular kinds of writing about reading and writing across the curriculum. (Mary Ehrenworth, Chris Lehman, and I have written a book detailing our thinking about the CCSS and the implications for teachers and for curriculum, *Pathways to the Common Core*, and I invite you to read that book for a more detailed discussion of this topic.) We've also taken priorities of the Common Core State Standards and imbued them into all our work, including an emphasis on close reading, text-based questioning, data-based instruction, reading like a writer, writing about texts, quick writes, and transference.

The Teachers College Reading and Writing Project is especially embedded in schools within New York State, which means that the frameworks New York State has adopted for accelerating achievement toward CCSS levels are part and parcel of these units. This includes:

- Attention to the level of cognitive challenge we provide students using Webb's depth of knowledge as a guide
- Reliance on curricular mapping design strategies
- Attention to Charlotte Danielson's teacher-effectiveness framework
- A focus on formative and summative assessments and data-based instruction

The work your students will do as you teach the units of study in this series and as you track and support their progress on the learning progressions that undergird this curriculum will provide them with the instruction, opportunities for practice, and goals they need to meet the CCSS for writing at their grade level. In fact, since we believe it is so important for every child to be able to meet those standards, we have made sure that every yearlong curriculum teaches students in ways that support standards-level work at the level *above* their grade level. This allows for accelerated progress for students who can make that progress and for extra time and scaffolding for those who need this to become proficient at the grade-level standard. The CCSS for middle school students are extremely high. We believe the best way to be sure students will be able to meet the demanding eighth-grade standards is for them to enter middle school already well on the way toward mastering the sixth-grade standards.

Because the units of study at each grade level support students working within the standards of the upcoming grade, these units of study support children becoming highly proficient, while also allowing youngsters who need more teaching and more practice to receive those extended opportunities to learn while still achieving proficiency. The units, then, help teachers and students to aim not only for grade level standards but also beyond them. Runners don't aim to stop at the finish line; they aim to run right through it, keeping up the pace until the finish line is well behind them. We, too, want to aim beyond the finish line—bringing every child with us as we do so.

Although this series does not take on the entire job of helping students meet the Common Core Reading, Speaking and Listening, and Language Standards, good writing instruction requires meeting many of these standards all the same, and you'll find the units help you do this. You'll see CCSS correlation charts aligned to each unit that will help you understand which of these other sets of standards these units help you meet and which will especially need attention in other times of the school day—in social studies or science, reading, and language/word study. The good news is that the work students do across the entire curriculum will be given a lift by the skills they develop within the writing workshop.

I discuss the CCSS in more depth in the next chapter.

This New Series Reflects Current Research and Knowledge

Since we published the first Units of Study series, knowledge of education has changed. The work of Danielson, Marzano, Webb, Wiggins, Hattie, and others has coalesced into new images and understandings of effective practice. Teachers are being assessed with new lenses in mind. Students' progress is now tracked with preassessments, formative assessments, and summative assessments. Somehow, all of that assessing must be synthesized into instruction that is more rigorous, more powerful, than ever—and that means the instruction needs to be more assessment-based and data driven as well as more cognitively demanding than ever.

Over the past few years, the Teachers College Reading and Writing Project has been the primary vehicle for professional development in more than a thousand schools, including high-need schools and high-performing private, charter, and public schools. These partnerships mean that we regularly help schools undergo quality review, develop and adopt CCSS–aligned performance assessments, use software systems to track student progress, and demonstrate to evaluators that instruction is data based and differentiated. Our deep involvement with all of this work has helped our own ideas evolve. The fruits of that labor are infused into these units of study.

THE AUTHORSHIP OF THIS SERIES

Although the text reads as if one teacher created and taught the minilessons, mid-workshop teachings, small groups, and shares, the creation and teaching was actually much more collaborative. Usually, before embarking on a project, the coauthors and I will have designed and taught scores, even hundreds, of units of study related to the topic of the unit book. Usually the work began with the coauthor and me working hard to develop a tentative plan for the entire unit. Implicit in such a document are literally hundreds of decisions, and our initial plans were always revised endlessly before becoming the backbone of the unit. During the early planning portion of the process, we'd decide on mentor texts and the like. Then, I'd usually draft the first few minilessons and the coauthor would pilot those minilessons in a few classrooms, and we'd work together to revise them. Then one of us would draft the bare bones of the next sessions, and again, others would chip in. The initial draft of the first bend usually went through four or five wholesale revisions, was taught several times, and was passed among a number of hands before it was close to being finished. Once the first bend had been written and taught, plans for the upcoming bend would be revised based on all that we'd learned, and then the process continued. I ended up revising at least half the books from head to toe again, later in the process.

In the same way, although the books read as if they draw on one classroom, depicting the true story of how that unit of study unfolded in that one classroom, in truth, the classroom that is depicted in these books is usually a composite classroom, and the kids' voices are captured or created from all the kids we've taught.

The series, then, stands on the shoulders of the Teachers College Reading and Writing Project community. The books have, in a sense, been coauthored by the entire staff of this professional development organization and by the children, teachers, principals, and superintendents who have become part of the community of practice, helping develop, pilot, and revise the ideas that fill the pages of these books.

Chapter 2

What Do the CCSS Say about Writing, and What Does This Mean for Us?

THIS SERIES IS BEING PUBLISHED just as the United States sets out on an effort to lift the level of literacy instruction across all our schools, making sure that students enter college and twenty-first-century careers ready to flourish. As I've written in our recent professional book, *Pathways to the Common Core* (2012), the Common Core State Standards are a big deal. Adopted by forty-five states and the District of Columbia so far, the standards represent the most sweeping reform of the K–12 curriculum that has ever occurred in this country. It is safe to say that across the entire history of American education, no single document has played a more influential role over what is taught in our schools. The standards are already shaping what is published, mandated, and tested in schools—and also what is marginalized and neglected. Any educator who wants to play a role in shaping what happens in schools, therefore, needs a deep understanding of these standards.

If I were asked to describe the two or three most striking features of the Common Core State Standards, one of the things I'd say straightaway is that the standards place a tremendous emphasis on writing. In effect, the standards refocus the nation on students' proficiency as writers. NCLB, the last large-scale reform movement in literacy, called for an emphasis on phonemic awareness, phonics, vocabulary, fluency, and comprehension. Writing was nowhere in the picture. In the Common Core State Standards, in contrast, writing is treated as an equal partner to reading, and more than this, writing is assumed to be *the* vehicle through which a great deal of the critical thinking, reading work, and reading assessment will occur. The CCSS, then, return writing to its place as one of the essentials of education.

In this chapter, I help you grasp the Common Core's rallying cry around writing and see how these units of study help you meet (and even, at times, exceed) these demands. This chapter looks specifically at:

- The standards' emphasis on three types of writing
- The relationship between the CCSS for writing and the Units of Study series

- The writing process described in the standards and taught in these units of study
- The standards' call for new levels of proficiency

In subsequent chapters in this guide, you'll see how the structure, focus, and content of the units align to—and are influenced by—the Common Core State Standards. You'll see the influence of the Common Core also as you read the individual lessons that lead students toward and beyond CCSS benchmarks.

THE STANDARD'S EMPHASIS ON THREE TYPES OF WRITING

In the prelude to the Common Core Standards, there is a section entitled "Key Features of the Standards." This synopsis emphasizes that although the writing process applies to all kinds of writing, different types of writing place different demands on students.

The standards are organized in a way that highlights grade-specific expectations for three broad types of writing. The first standard delineates expectations for opinion and argument writing; the second, for information writing; and the third, for narrative writing. Although these three standards represent just under a third of the ten standards, if one were to count the pages devoted to the writing standards and count the pages devoted to explicating the three types of writing, one would find that these first three standards occupy fully half of the CCSS for writing. (The later standards illuminate how students should do the work of the first three standards. For example, students presumably will use the writing process detailed in standard 5, the writing process standard, as they write the argument, information, and narrative texts described in standards 1–3.)

It is interesting to note that the standards refer to these as *types* of writing and not as *genres*. This makes sense because within any one type of writing, one can lodge many different genres of writing. In the New Standards Project, an earlier effort to create nationwide standards, the committee of twenty (including me) who wrote those standards wrestled with the issue of *kinds* versus *structures* versus *types* versus *genres* of writing and came to the decision that the whole world of writing could be divided into five (not three)

kinds of writing: narrative, information, functional and procedural, persuasion and argument, and poetry. The Common Core State Standards' divisions are roughly in line with those earlier ones, although functional and procedural writing are now combined with information writing, and poetry is excluded.

You might, with colleagues, try jotting down the genres you would put under these major categories, and then consider how often your students have opportunities to engage in each of the three main types of writing. You will probably come up with lists like these.

- **Narrative writing:** personal narrative, fiction, historical fiction, fantasy, narrative memoir, biography, narrative nonfiction
- **Persuasive/opinion/argument writing:** persuasive letter, petition, persuasive speech, review, personal essay, persuasive essay, literary essay, historical essay, editorial, op-ed column, research-based argument essay
- **Informational and functional/procedural writing:** how-to book, directions, recipe, lab report, fact sheet, news article, feature article, blog, website, report, analytic memo, research report, nonfiction book

The CCSS and Narrative Texts

Although the sequence of the first three anchor standards for writing starts with argument writing and ends with narrative writing, learners grow into these genres in just the opposite direction. Human beings grow up on narratives, on stories. We come to know our own parents by hearing their stories of growing up. We make friendships by sharing the stories of our lives. We get jobs and scholarships by telling the stories of our studies and careers. We stay in touch by regaling each other with the news of our comings and goings. We plan and daydream and work and worry in narrative; we recall and remember in narrative. We comprehend fiction and biography and narrative nonfiction by synthesizing what we read on one page, another, and another into narratives that we hope are coherent and satisfying.

Narratives are important not only because they are, as researcher Barbara Hardy says, the primary mode of knowing ("Narrative as a Primary Act of Mind" in *The Cool Web: The Patterns of Children's Reading*, 1977) but also because they are an essential component in almost every other kind of writing.

Listen to TED talks—models of persuasive and informative speaking—and you will find that mostly, those speeches are mosaics of stories. Read a terrific informational text, and you'll find that you are reading stories.

If you try to understand the narrative writing standards by turning immediately to the grade you teach and reading the descriptors for that grade, you'll probably find the expectations to be overwhelming. Before you dismiss the standards as unrealistically high, you need to read them in an entirely different fashion. Start with kindergarten, and read those grade-level skills for narrative. Imagine a very simple story that meets those descriptors. Then reread just the first subitem in the kindergarten narrative standard before looking to the right to note what added work first-graders are expected to do in narrative writing. The added work won't be much—and that will prove true as you progress through the narrative expectations. By proceeding in this way, reading in a horizontal fashion, setting the descriptors for each skill from one grade alongside those for the next grade and noting the new work that is added at each subsequent grade, you'll come to understand the trajectory along which writers can travel. It is this trajectory that we used when designing the narrative units in this series (and it is the information and opinion trajectories that we used for the information and opinion units). Using these incremental steps, this steady progression will, in fact, make the writing standards something that students can achieve, especially if they have the opportunity to grow up within a strong writing curriculum.

The CCSS and Opinion/Argument Texts

Argument writing is a *big deal* in the Common Core State Standards. In fact, the writers include an entire section in Appendix A titled "The Special Place of Argument in the Standards" to emphasize their strong belief in argumentation. The section begins: "While all three text types are important, the Standards put particular emphasis on students' ability to write sound arguments on substantive topics and issues, as this ability is critical to college and career readiness" (2010, 24). To support their argument, the authors refer to statements by college professors who each make additional claims for the centrality of argument in universities. Gerald Graff, for example, claims that the university is largely "an argument culture" (*Clueless in Academe*, 2003, 24). It is with

this particular vision of university life that the standards writers mapped their expectations for argument writing from high school graduation backward.

This belief in the essential nature of argumentation, at least on the part of the writers of the standards, colors many areas of the CCSS document. There is a push for logical reasoning, analysis of claims, and reliance on clear evidence and evaluation of sources throughout the document.

The pace at which the opinion and argument standards develop is brisk when you study them longitudinally. Kindergarten and first grade begin simply enough, expecting a student to introduce a topic and supply some opinion for it, perhaps with a reason. But then in second grade, the student is already expected to structure his or her writing in support of his or her claim. In fact, in some respects, the expectations for second-grade argument writing, at least in terms of the text of the standards, seem to extend well beyond those for the other two writing types. In second-grade information writing, the main emphasis seems to be only that the text includes a variety of details, whereas the expectations for argument writing are more extensive.

There are three important ideas that will help you study the Common Core standards for argument writing: the progression of expectations for opinion and argument writing is steep; the K–5 emphasis on opinion writing gives way to a 6–12 emphasis on argument writing (which includes counterargument and more critical weighing of sources, evidence, and logic); and writing arguments eventually includes using and evaluating sources, and using this analysis to power convincing arguments. The opinion and argument units in this series support this full progression of skills so that students develop research-based argument writing skills in fifth grade.

The CCSS and Information Texts

To understand the Common Core State Standards for information writing, it is helpful to pause for a moment and think of all the information writing that students do in school. Although research reports and nonfiction books spring to mind right away, this category of writing is far broader than that. Information writing includes entries, Post-it® notes, summaries written in response to reading, lab reports, math records, and descriptions of and reflections on movies, field trips, and books. Under the umbrella of the broad category, one also finds the answers students write in response to questions at the end of textbook chapters or questions discussed in class. The CCSS authors highlight the breadth of this type of writing in Appendix A.

> Informational/explanatory writing includes a wide array of genres, including academic genres such as literary analyses, scientific and historical reports, summaries, and précis writing as well as forms of workplace and functional writing such as instructions, manuals, memos, reports, applications, and résumés. (23)

In essence, the skills required to write information texts are not just writing skills, they are learning skills. Let's clarify something before diving much further into this topic: although the rhetoric around the Common Core suggests that the standards call for exponentially increasing the amount of information writing done in school, this depends on the amount of writing teachers have done all along. The truth is that for teachers in grades K–5, the Common Core standards ask only that one-third of all the writing that students do across the entire day be information writing. That is, most of the writing in science, social studies, art, and computers all qualifies as information writing.

We think it's important to note that for many schools, the challenge is not the expectation that students devote a greater percentage of their writing to texts that fall under the broad umbrella of information writing (it is already commonplace for one-third of the writing that students do to be information writing). Rather, the challenge is that the Common Core expects students to apply the same standard of craftsmanship to information writing as they do to short stories, memoirs, and essays. That is, traditionally, when students wrote about reading (whether literature or history or science), the goal was for them to show that they had done the reading, gleaned the necessary knowledge, and

For students to become highly skilled at specific types of writing, and be held accountable for meeting CCSS expectations, they need opportunities for repeated practice, not only within a unit of study but also across units and grades."

developed some thoughts. Prior to the arrival of the CCSS, it wasn't typical for their information writing to be held up to the same standards as essays and short stories. Now, a reader of the CCSS can quickly see that across all three kinds of writing, there is a parallel emphasis on writing in clear structures, on elaborating with specific information, on writing with details and examples, and on synthesizing the text so that the entire text advances key ideas or themes.

THE RELATIONSHIP BETWEEN THE CCSS FOR WRITING AND THE UNITS OF STUDY SERIES

The standards, you'll recall, focus on expectations and not methods. They detail what students should know and be able to do; they do not specify practices that teachers must use to teach students the skills necessary to meet those expectations. School districts and teachers are left to decide on an instructional program that will elevate the level of student writing so that all (or most) students reach these ambitious expectations. One can't help but think that an effort to meet the standards will require a planned, sequential, explicit writing program, with instruction that gives students repeated opportunities to practice each kind of writing and to receive explicit feedback at frequent intervals.

This new series offers one such program. The units of study in this series offer at least one highly developed unit devoted to each type of writing at each grade level. Within each unit of study, students are expected to write more than one piece (and sometimes a multitude of pieces). The fact that students are given repeated opportunities to produce a particular kind of writing is important if we are going to hold students accountable to meet CCSS expectations. For anyone to become highly skilled at a specific type of writing, that person needs opportunities for repeated practice. In this series, these opportunities are given not only within a unit of study but also across units of study and grades.

Progression and Transference across Units and Grades

Across all of the units, there is a continual emphasis on transference. For example, after students write persuasive speeches, they study another kind of persuasive writing—petitions—and ask, "How many of the strategies that we learned when writing persuasive speeches are applicable also when writing petitions?" This inquiry leads students to plunge right into the work of writing petitions without needing an elaborate introduction. The very design of the Common Core emphasizes the fact that students will be able to reach high-level expectations when skills are built on as students proceed through the grades. In this series, the cohesion across units means that skills that are introduced in one grade level are then recalled and developed in later units of study.

This development occurs within a type of writing and also across the full gamut of writing. That is, the standards' expectations for one type of writing, at a grade level, are echoed in the other two types of writing. If students are expected to end their essays by referring back not only to the last paragraph but to their entire essay, they'll encounter parallel expectations for their endings when writing narratives and information texts. It is helpful for students if teachers say, "You know the work you have been doing to make sure that the ending of your essay relates to the whole text, not just to the last bit of it? Well, when you write fiction, there are similar expectations for your endings. Let me explain and show you what I mean."

You will want to study the standards so that you understand the way that expectations grow each year, with students being expected to produce work that stands on the shoulders of the preceding year. For example, first-graders are expected to write opinion pieces in which they introduce the topic of the book they are writing about, state an opinion, supply a reason to support that opinion, and provide some sense of closure. By sixth grade, students are expected to write arguments (not opinions) to support claims with clear reasons and relevant evidence. In these arguments, students are expected to introduce the claim(s) and organize the reasons and evidence clearly; support claim(s) with clear reasons and relevant evidence, using credible sources to demonstrate an understanding of the topic or text; use words, phrases, and

clauses to clarify the relationships among claims and reasons; establish a formal style; and provide a concluding statement or section that follows from the argument presented.

The standards not only describe the progression of skill development expected to occur across grades in a curriculum in which one grade builds on the next, but they also provide annotated exemplar texts to illustrate what these pieces of writing might look like and to answer the question, "How good is good enough?" When looking at the pieces provided as illustrations of one type of writing or another, it is important to note that even the pieces selected as exemplars do not adhere to all of the defining characteristics of a genre. For readers who are accustomed to teaching in writing workshops, it will be clear after just a glance that most of the exemplar pieces in Appendix B emerged out of writing workshop classrooms.

Exemplar pieces are important, and although the standards include a random sampling of some exemplars, they don't show information, opinion, and narrative pieces that illustrate each of the standards they detail. This series does provide those benchmark texts in *Writing Pathways: Performance Assessments and Learning Progressions, K–5*. Of course, once you teach these units, you will have files of student work from previous years that you can draw on, and you will want to do so.

If you are by any chance operating in isolation, a sort of lone champion of writing in your school, I encourage you to reach out in every possible way to your colleagues. Your influence on one class of writers will be multiplied tenfold if students receive instruction each year that builds on prior years, that makes sense to students, and that holds them accountable to transferring and applying their skills. To reach the Common Core standards, children will benefit from writing becoming a schoolwide vision.

Writing across the Curriculum

Although the expectations for writing that are embedded in the CCSS mostly align to the research and teaching that the Teachers College Reading and Writing Project has been engaged in for the past thirty years, there have been important new challenges as well. First and foremost, the CCSS emphasize that writing needs to occur in disciplines and be supported by all teachers. Writing cannot be the province only of the language arts classroom. As part of this, the CCSS spotlight the importance of high standards for writing that is done within the content areas. Children need to be able to structure their research reports, synthesize information, and explore the ramifications of evidence. This means that young people need explicit instruction and lots of opportunities to write within social studies and science, and to develop as writers of information and opinion texts. This series contains research-based units that are embedded in the content areas as well as in the writing workshop.

A word about balance. The standards not only define and describe the three kinds of writing and show how students' work within each of those kinds of writing should progress across the years, but they also call for a distribution of writing experiences that gives students roughly equal amounts of time and instruction in argument, informative, and narrative writing.

In the Common Core, the discussion of the distribution of writing between these types of texts is situated under the subheading of "Shared Responsibility" (4) as part of an emphasis on writing instruction belonging in the hands of all disciplines and every teacher. So, if fifth-grade students are expected to write narratives 35% of the time, information texts 35% of the time, and opinions/arguments 30% of the time, the balance between the three types of writing is expected to occur across math, social studies, science, gym, and music, as well as during writing workshop itself. Presumably, a good deal of the information writing will occur in science (lab reports), in math (math journals reflecting on the students' processes), in social studies (summaries of texts read, responses to questions asking students to synthesize information from several sources), and in reading (reading notebook entries, quick analytic jottings, preparations for partnership and book club conversations). This suggests that the CCSS recommend that a large portion of the writing done during the literacy or language arts block be narrative and opinion writing, although in this series, we support an equal distribution between the three types of writing.

The implications of the writing standards are clear. Writing must become part of the bill of rights for all students. Just as it would be unacceptable for a K–5 teacher to say, "Math's not really my thing," so too, in the world of the Common Core, it will be indefensible for a teacher, of any subject, to say, "Writing is not really my cup of tea."

Teaching to and above the Standards

Throughout the series, you will see that the teaching often reflects standards one grade level above. There are several reasons for this. First, teaching

beyond the standards gives students the opportunity to reach toward the goal of working at highly proficient levels. Then too, as described previously, this means that students have additional time, when needed, to develop the skills they are expected to demonstrate. And finally, our research in thousands of writing classrooms has suggested that there are some places where the Common Core State Standards underestimate what K–5 students can do. This is especially true in the primary grades, where the writing standards progress more slowly than in the upper grades. This means that there are instances in which expectations accelerate at a rate that we believe is unrealistically steep—most notably between sixth and seventh grade. Our suggestion, then, is for K–5 teachers to aim to send students to sixth grade already having met many of the sixth-grade standards. This positions students to leave eighth grade meeting or exceeding CCSS expectations.

THE WRITING PROCESS DESCRIBED IN THE STANDARDS AND TAUGHT IN THESE UNITS OF STUDY

While there is some dispute in this nation about methods for teaching *reading*, there is less dispute about methods for teaching *writing*. This is probably because while we don't have many public figures who are readers, there have been thousands of writers who have made their process public. There is near universal agreement that writers engage in a process of collecting, drafting, revising, and editing. You can see writers' drafts, with their many revisions, in library collections, online, and in books such as the Author at Work series. From Mark Twain to Bob Woodward, from novelists to journalists, writers draft and revise—sometimes rapidly and on the run, and sometimes over extended periods. It's no surprise, then, that the standards embrace the widely accepted writing process.

Writing standard 5 describes the writing process, and standard 10 describes the need to write routinely as part of that process. Both standards will be an integral part of attaining all the other writing standards as well. The grade-level specifics of anchor standard 5 are almost the same across all the grades. This standard says that students should be able to "develop and strengthen writing as needed by planning, revising, [and] editing" (18), with expectations for revision and independence increasing with age. Anchor standard 10 calls for students to "write routinely over extended time frames (time for research,

WHAT DO THE CCSS SAY ABOUT WRITING, AND WHAT DOES THIS MEAN FOR US?

15

reflection, and revision) and shorter time frames (a single sitting or a day or two)" (18). These are not low expectations! You'll find, as you dive deeper into these units, that tremendous attention is paid to on-demand writing at the start and end of each unit, and to students producing a volume of writing. Writing with velocity matters, as does writing to deadline.

Efficiency and fluency also matter. These skills come with writing often, which the standards call for students to do. "Write routinely" means to make writing a habit. Even noted writers describe how they have to push themselves to ensure that they write every day. Novelist Margaret Atwood, who has published dozens of fiction and nonfiction books and has received almost every known award for her writing, claims, "The fact is the blank pages inspire me with terror. What will I put on them? Will it be good enough? Will I have to throw it out? The trick is to sit at the desk anyway, every day" (Donald Murray, *Shoptalk: Learning to Write with Writers*, 1990, 72). It is not surprising that the standards emphasize writing often. Writing is just like any other practice—playing piano, running, knitting. The more opportunity you have for practice, the better you get. In these units, a day does not go by that your children are not writing. Across a week, they will write many pages. Inevitably, they will get better, faster, more fluent, more efficient, and more powerful.

A writing routine does not just come with sitting down to write, however. A writing routine involves understanding what it means to work at your writing. Writing anchor standard 5 states that writers will "develop and strengthen writing as needed by planning, revising, editing, rewriting, or trying a new approach" (18). The CCSS are closely aligned, then, with the practices researched by Pulitzer prize–winning journalist Don Murray, documented in *A Writer Teaches Writing* (2003). Murray described how journalists learn, even when writing to deadline, to revise on the run, to try out different leads and endings, and to consider and reconsider each word, comma, and sentence structure to convey precise meaning. In other words, they know that writing is a process.

Volume is also related to rate, and the standards are very specific about the expectations for production. Fourth-graders are expected to produce a

minimum of one typed page in a sitting, and fifth-graders, a minimum of two typed pages in a sitting. We have seen students sit down to write an on-demand piece at the end of a unit of study and regularly produce that much writing. When they know a lot about that which they are writing, their pencils will fly. When they are used to writing often, their fingers and minds will be ready. That level of production comes with practice.

This has led teachers to look closely at their schedules for writing, following a student across a week, seeing how much time is actually available for that student to write, and paying attention to how much writing he or she produces during one sitting. In every school where kids become powerful writers, they have extended time to write, and they write daily. Don Graves, pioneer reformer in writing instruction for children, often said that if writers couldn't return to a piece of writing at least three times a week, it wasn't worth doing at all. The kids would just be too far away from their writing to remain committed to it (Graves, *Writing: Teachers and Children at Work*, 2003).

If you've ever practiced piano scales, you know that after a long stretch away from the piano, when you first sit down your fingers are slow. It's the same if you haven't exercised in a while or if you haven't picked up knitting needles in five years. You know the skills, but your legs or fingers don't respond with the speed they once did. On the other hand, as you begin to knit or run or play piano or write, you'll find that for every day you do it, the sheer discipline of moving your pen across the page or your fingers across the keyboard, you will become faster and more fluent.

A note about typing versus handwriting: in most schools, students are writing on paper, not computers, because computers are expensive. You'll see that most of the K–5 student pieces that are in Appendix C of the standards are handwritten. That said, if your students have easy access to technology, it is important to help them develop those skills. It appears upcoming high-stake assessments will be conducted via computers. You'll see, in the units of study, publishing options include podcasts, blogs, and other digital media, but ultimately, we've left the decision to highlight digital technology mostly in your hands.

THE STANDARDS CALL FOR NEW LEVELS OF PROFICIENCY

While the CCSS are notable for requiring an equal division of time between three kinds of writing and for frequent opportunities to engage in the writing process, the most remarkable thing about the CCSS is the call for high levels of proficiency. The expectations are not high for the younger grades, but they escalate between grades 5–8. In grade 5, the lead paragraph to a narrative story should "orient the reader by establishing a situation and introducing a narrator and/or characters; organize an event sequence that unfolds naturally" (20). So the writer is supposed to introduce the conflict and its context, introduce the narrator and the characters, and launch a sequence of events. And all of that just describes the opening few lines to a story! Many teachers no doubt think, "Could I write like that, with that much power and concision, let alone teach an eleven-year-old to write like that?" The expectations are especially high when one looks at the eighth-grade sample texts included in Appendix C.

Let's look at an example of a piece of writing from Appendix C (see http://www.corestandards.org/assets/Appendix_C.pdf) that represents what kindergartners should be able to do as information writers:

> To day befor We had riyda groos Mrs. John red us a strorry a baowt frogs. We had to riet a baowt frogs. We haf a tadpol in the sciens sentr. It has 2 bac ligs and wen it has 2 frunt ligs its tal disuprs and it can not yet wen its moot is chajn. Then the scknn gets to little and the frogs pol off thrr scknn an thaa eyt it. Saum of the frogs bloo baubools. Frogs lad eggs that look like jele and the fish yet some but some hach to tadpoos. It gros bigr and bigr and bigr.

The child has drawn on multiple sources of information, including observation and a text that was read aloud. The writer uses detail ("when it has 2 front legs its tail disappears") and precise and even domain-specific language (*tadpole, hatch*) to describe the life cycle of a frog. The writer makes comparisons ("eggs that look like jelly") and uses repetition for dramatic effect ("bigger and bigger and bigger").

The pieces in the appendix are not all of even quality. Sometimes one type of writing at a grade level will represent what we might think are relatively low standards, while another piece, like this one, seems high. You'll need to look between the descriptors, the grade-level specifics in the standards—which tend to be rather low, especially in kindergarten and through fourth grade—and the pieces themselves to try to build a coherent vision of proficiency levels if you're interested in doing this work. By the end of the year, you should be able to create your own Appendix C, with student exemplars from your community and curriculum.

The expectations for writing in the CCSS are also carried by anchor standard 4. At every grade level, starting in grade 3, standard 4 says that students are expected to "produce clear and coherent writing in which the development and organization are appropriate to task, purpose, and audience" (18). Note that a spotlight is placed on clarity and structure, as opposed to vividness or voice. This is interesting to us because we have often felt that one can look at various theories about writing instruction and ask, "Does this prioritize the sort of lush writing one finds in picture books, novels, and poems, or does it prioritize the lucid, clear writing that one finds in William Strunk and E. B. White's *Elements of Style*?" The CCSS lean toward the latter.

The Standards' Emphasis on the Importance of Writing for Very Young Students

The important thing about the primary writing standards is that all of the skills considered to be essential for a student graduating from high school have their beginnings in the primary grades. The standards do not suggest that young kids write only stories and older students write just essays. Instead, kindergartners, like twelfth-graders, are given repeated practice in writing their opinions and then supporting those opinions with reasons. Kindergartners, like twelfth-graders, draft, revise, edit, and publish their writing. Implicit in the CCSS is the presence of a coherent, synthesized K–12 curriculum. A child who has been learning narrative craft for thirteen years should, by the end of twelfth grade, be extraordinarily skilled, ready to spin an anecdote from his or her own story into an engaging college essay or scholarship application. A child who wrote opinions in the primary grades, then moved to carefully constructed arguments in middle school, will be ready to embark on learning the skills needed to contextualize an argument, acknowledge and refute the counterargument, and analyze the research base and bias of sources.

Although this guide is for upper-elementary-grade teachers, the CCSS' message to K–12 teachers matters to you. For you to do your job, it is important that writing instruction in your school start in kindergarten. In thousands of schools across the nation, teachers start the kindergarten year by saying to children, "In this classroom, each one of you will be an author. Each one of you will write stories and letters and instructions and songs and all-about books." Although this teaching has spread like wildfire, it is still far from the norm. In the majority of classrooms, kindergarten is a time for socialization, for learning the alphabet, for perhaps copying the whole-class text with an emphasis on penmanship. The Common Core State Standards convey a crystal clear message opposed to this practice. The message is this: kindergartners can write. They can not only invent their own spellings and write with fluency and power but also write long, well-developed, shapely texts.

Look again at that sample piece for kindergarten included in Appendix C.

To day befor We had riyda groos Mrs. John red us a strorry a baowt frogs. We had to riet a baowt frogs. We haf a tadpol in the sciens sentr. It has 2 bac ligs and wen it has 2 frunt ligs its tal disuprs and it can not yet wen its moot is chajn. Then the scknn gets to little and the frogs pol off thrr scknn an thaa eyt it. Saum of the frogs bloo baubools. Frogs lad eggs that look like jele and the fish yet some but some hach to tadpoos. It gros bigr and bigr and bigr.

Kindergarten teachers debate whether this piece is a realistic goal for all kindergarten children and they are right to do so. But the point that matters is that the CCSS say clearly that in order for upper-elementary teachers to bring children to standards, the teaching of writing needs to be a whole-school priority. The standards acknowledge it will be hard for students to achieve the high level of craft that is expected of them if teachers haven't been moving them steadily along a progressing curriculum, extending their skills in each type of writing each year, and giving them clear expectations for their writing and feedback toward meeting those expectations. After all, in math, teachers ensure that students move through the grade levels with the essential skills that teachers have agreed on. That same focus on writing as content, as a set of skills, will move grade levels of students forward, rather than simply those students who happened to get this teacher or that.

Writing will need to be given its due, starting in kindergarten and continuing throughout the grades. Teachers will need to assess and teach writing, to track students' progress, and to plan interventions for those students who need extra help in writing. In short, writing will need to be treated just as math has been treated in the past. The standards give you a powerful voice in advocating for a writing curriculum and for time in the schedule for children to work on their writing.

The Common Core has been written, but the plan for implementing the Common Core has not. As challenging as it must have been to write this document and to finesse its adoption, that work is nothing compared to the work of teaching in ways that bring all students to these ambitious expectations. As you know by now, we've built these units intending to support you in doing just that.

Chapter 3

The Essentials of Writing Instruction

WHENEVER I WORK WITH EDUCATORS IN A SCHOOL, school district, city, or country, I make a point of trying to learn about the vision guiding the approach to teaching writing. I ask, "What is the Bill of Rights that guides your work with your students as writers?" When people look quizzical, I rephrase my question. "When a child enters your school, what is the promise that you make to the child and her parents about the writing education that she will receive?" I point out that chances are good that in math, the school essentially promises that child, "Whether or not your teacher likes math, you'll be taught math every day. You won't need to be lucky to get a teacher who teaches math. And the course of study that you receive from one teacher won't be all that different from what you'll receive from another teacher."

Given that writing is one of those subjects that affects a learner's ability to succeed in every other subject, the promise a school makes to youngsters as writers probably shouldn't be that different from the promise made to children as mathematicians. In this chapter, I share the essentials—the *bottom line conditions*, as we've come to call them—that school systems that provide effective writing instruction to all children have in common. These school districts agree that the following conditions are important.

Writing needs to be taught like any other basic skill, with explicit instruction and ample opportunity for practice. Almost every day, every student in grades K–5 needs between fifty and sixty minutes for writing instruction and writing.

Although teachers must make decisions about their own teaching, no teacher on her own can decide not to teach math nor can she decide to teach math by assigning it across every subject area. Asking children to add up the number of pages they've read or to count the minutes until school is dismissed wouldn't suffice as a substitute for a math curriculum. Yet in some districts it is acceptable for teachers to say, "I just teach writing across the curriculum. Kids summarize their *Magic Treehouse* book, for example, or answer questions about a film about sea life, and we call that writing instruction."

I often point out to administrators that although there is no doubt that writing must be a part of every subject, when a teacher describes her writing instruction by saying, "We do writing across the curriculum," I know that teacher is probably saying, "I don't explicitly teach writing." Assigning children to write texts—a thank-you letter to the visiting scientist or a new ending to the whole-class book—is not the same as providing students with a planned, coherent curriculum in writing.

It has become increasingly clear that children's success in many disciplines is utterly reliant on their ability to write. And writing, like reading and math, is a skill that develops over time. Because of this, more and more schools are recognizing that children deserve writing to be a subject that is taught and studied just like reading or math; in thousands of schools around the world, writing is a subject that is taught just like any other essential skill. In these schools, in grades 3–5, the day involves an hour for reading, an hour for writing, and more time for language study.

It is necessary that during writing time, children write for stretches of time. Just as learners become skilled at playing an instrument or swimming or playing tennis or reading by doing those things, writing, too, is learned through practice. As my sons' tennis teacher says, "Success in tennis has everything to do with the number of balls hit." Similarly, success in reading directly correlates with the number of hours spent reading. John Guthrie's study ("Teaching for Literacy Engagement," in *Journal of Literacy Research*, 2004) illustrates that fourth-graders who read at the second-grade level spend a half-hour a day reading, and fourth-graders who read at the eighth-grade level spend four and a half hours a day reading. Success in writing, like success in reading or tennis or swimming, directly relates to the amount of time a person spends writing and rewriting. This means that day after day, children need to write. They need to write for long stretches of time—for something like thirty or forty minutes of each day's writing workshop. And it means that volume and stamina matter.

Students date each day's writing, and all the writing stays in the students' notebooks or folders until the unit of study culminates in a publishing party.

> *"It has become increasingly clear that children's success in many disciplines is reliant on their ability to write."*

This allows teachers, literacy coaches, and principals to look through the students' writer's notebooks and their folders and see the work any student produced on Monday, Tuesday, Wednesday, and so forth.

Writers write. A wonderful thing about writing is it's immediately visible. This allows a school system to hold itself accountable for ensuring that every child has the opportunity and the responsibility to write every day.

Youngsters deserve to write for real, to write the kinds of texts that they see in the world—nonfiction chapter books, persuasive letters, stories, lab reports, reviews, poems—and to write for an audience of readers, not just for the teacher's red pen.

Donald Murray, the Pulitzer prize–winning writer who is widely regarded as the father of the writing process, recalls the piano lessons he was given as a child. The school system announced that anyone wanting to learn to play the piano should report to the cafeteria after school. Murray recalls his palpable excitement: at last, he was going to learn to make those beautiful melodies! In the cafeteria, children sat in rows, facing the front. Each child was given a cardboard keyboard and shown how to lay his or her hands on it so as to "play" notes. Children pressed their cardboard keyboards, but there was no music, no melody. Murray left and never returned.

Young people deserve opportunities to write real writing; this means that instead of writing merely "pieces" and "assignments," children need to write in all the genres that exist in the world. A child should know that he or she is writing *something*—a nonfiction book, a book review, an editorial, a lab report, a fantasy—that writers write and readers read. The child needs to know, too, that others have written this same kind of thing and that one of the best ways to learn is to study the work others have made, asking, "What did he do that I could try in my writing?"

Youngsters not only deserve daily opportunities to write particular kinds of things—to write *something* that exists in the world—they also deserve opportunities to write for *someone*—for readers who will respond to what they have written. They deserve to write knowing that their writing stands a good chance of being read by readers. Otherwise how will young writers learn that writing well involves aiming to create an effect? Craft and deliberate choice in writing are the result of thinking, as one writes, "They'll laugh at this part!" or "This will make them want to know all about it." To write with this sense of agency, children need to see readers respond to their writing. They need to share their writing with partners, to read it aloud to small groups, and to have people respond as readers do—laughing at the funny parts, gasping at the sad parts, leaning forward to learn more.

Giving children opportunities to write *something* (a letter, a speech) for *someone* (a younger class, a grandfather) makes it likely that writing will engage children and they will feel what they are doing is real, credible, and substantial. Children should not be asked to learn to play music on cardboard keyboards or to learn to write on ditto sheets.

Writers write to put meaning onto the page. Young people will especially invest themselves in their writing if they write about subjects that are important to them. The easiest way to support investment in writing is to teach children to choose their own topics most of the time.

Try this. Pick up a pen and write a few sentences about the sequence of actions you did just before picking up this book. Do it on paper or in your mind.

Now pause and try something different. Think about a moment in your life that for some reason really affected you. It might be the tiniest of moments, but it gave you a lump in your throat; it made your heart skip. The last time you saw someone. The time you realized you could actually do that thing you'd been longing to do. Write (or mentally think through) the story of that indelible moment. On the page (or just in your mind's eye), try to capture the essence of that bit of life.

Or try this. Think of a subject on which you are an expert. If you were to teach a class on a topic, what would it be? What if that course was done through writing—what would the first lesson be? How would you start it?

You will find that picking up your pen and writing a few sentences about the sequence of actions you just did—a kind of writing in which you throw out any old words—is absolutely unlike the other kind of writing in which you reach for the precise words that will capture something important to you. For children to learn to write and grow as writers, it is absolutely essential that they are invested in their writing and that they care about writing well.

Students (indeed, all of us) are far more apt to be invested if they are writing about subjects they know and care about and if they are writing for real, responsive readers.

It is hard to imagine an argument against letting students choose their own topics for most of the writing they do in the writing workshop. When children are writing as part of a study of floating and sinking or weather, then of course teachers will channel some of their writing to specific subtopics within those units. But if the youngsters are working specifically on their writing skills, they'll work their hardest if they can choose their own subjects. Although the craft, strategies, and qualities of good writing and the processes of writing vary depending on whether someone is writing an editorial or an information book, good writing does not vary based on whether the information book is teaching about the kinds of stones in a riverbed or the kinds of dogs in a dog show. Teachers can gather the entire class together and teach them about that kind of writing—for example, the importance of detail or elaboration—knowing the instruction will be equally relevant to children who are engaged in writing about a wide array of subjects. (And there are advantages for suggesting that the whole class work for a period of time within a particular shared genre.)

The easiest way to help children love writing is to invite them to write about subjects they care about. When children have the opportunity and responsibility to choose their own subjects, they are not only much more apt to be invested in their writing, but they are also much more likely to know quite a bit about their topics. In addition, they can learn what it means to rediscover subjects through the process of writing about them.

Children deserve to be explicitly taught how to write. Instruction matters—and this includes instruction in spelling and conventions as well as in the qualities and strategies of good writing.

It is not enough to simply turn down the lights, turn on the music, and say to students, "Write." Nor is it okay to take anything that they produce and say, "You are an author!" It is not enough for youngsters to have time each day to crank out genre-less, audience-less, model-less, revision-less journal entries. It is not enough for children to be assigned to do this or that writing task. Writers need instruction. Writing improves in a palpable, dramatic fashion when students are given explicit instruction, lots of time to write, clear goals, and powerful feedback.

For example, if a child is writing an information book about history, that child may not discover on her own that it often helps to take notes in the form of a timeline, ordering the events even in the early stages of the writing. Then again, if a writer is stalled at the starting line of a piece, staring at the blank page, it can make a gigantic difference to teach that writer to rehearse for writing by teaching all about the topic to someone else.

I can walk into a classroom, look over children's writing, and know immediately whether children are being taught to write because strong, clear instruction dramatically and visibly affects student writing. When teachers explicitly teach the qualities, habits, and strategies of effective writing, that writing becomes better—and the improvement is evident within days and weeks, not just months.

One of the powerful things about writing instruction is that a good deal of it is multileveled. Say a writer is writing an information text about weather. If that writer has piled all that he or she knows onto a random assortment of sections, chances are good that it will make an enormous difference to suggest the writer think carefully about what the sections of his text should be and how to arrange them. A child who labors to write a few pages a day and a child who easily writes reams can benefit equally from that instruction. Both children, too, can look at a published information book to notice what the author has done that he or she could emulate. Actually, most strategies and qualities of good writing are multileveled. Some children will spell better than others, some will use more complex sentence structures than others, but many of the skills and strategies of skilled writing are within reach of every writer.

Children deserve the opportunity and instruction necessary for them to cycle through the writing process as they write: rehearsing, drafting, revising, editing, and publishing their writing.

The scientific method is widely regarded as so fundamental to science that children use it whether they are studying sinking and floating in kindergarten or friction and inertia in high school. In a similar way, the writing process is fundamental to all writing; therefore, it is important that children of every age receive frequent opportunities to rehearse, draft, revise, and edit their writing.

The important thing to realize is that teaching youngsters the process of writing is not the same as teaching them the names of presidents. The point is not for them to be able to parrot back the steps of writing well. The reason it is important for children to know the writing process is that when they aspire to write something, knowing the process is like knowing the recipe. For example, if a child is going to write an information article about presidential elections, her first concern should probably not be "What is my first sentence?" Instead, she'd do well to think first, "How does an article like this tend to go?" and "What kinds of structures could be good to use to organize this text?"

Of course, becoming at home with the process of writing is not unlike becoming at home with the process of doing long division or of solving word problems. It takes repeated practice. One learns and becomes more efficient over time. Things that once took a long time become quicker, more internalized, and more automatic.

This means that most of the time, it is useful for children to have opportunities to plan for and rehearse writing, to flash-draft, and to reread their rough draft, thinking, "How can I make this even better?" Feedback from a reader can help a writer imagine ways to improve the draft. A writer will always write with the conventions that are easily under his control, but once a text is almost ready for readers, the writer will want to edit it, taking extra care to make the text clearer and more correct. Often the writer will use outside assistance—from a partner or teacher—to edit.

Writers read. For children to write well, they need opportunities to read and to hear texts read, and to read as insiders, studying what other authors have done that they too could try.

Any effective writing curriculum acknowledges the importance of writers being immersed in powerful writing—whether in literature or another kind of text. Children learn to write from being engrossed in and affected by texts other authors have written. They need the sounds and power of good literature and strong nonfiction texts to seep into their bones. They need a sense of how an effective bit of persuasion can sway readers, for the way a poem can make a reader gasp and be still.

Children especially need opportunities to read as writers. Imagine that you were asked to write a foreword for this book. My hunch is that you'd likely do what I did when Georgia Heard asked me to write my first foreword ever. I pulled books from my shelf and searched for forewords. I found half a dozen and read them ravenously. "How does a foreword really go?" I asked. Children, too, deserve the chance to read like writers. I'll never forget the first-grader who wrote in the foreword to his own book, "If you like this book, you get a prize. If you don't like it, you get mud."

By studying the work of other authors, students not only develop a sense of what it is they are trying to make but also learn the conventions of that particular kind of text. Poets leave white space, how-to writers record steps, storytellers convey the passage of time. All writers care that the sound of their words matches the tone of their meaning. All writers care that they choose precisely right words. By studying texts that resemble those they are trying to write, children learn the tools of their trade.

Children need clear goals and frequent feedback. They need to hear ways their writing is getting better and to know what their next steps might be.

Research by John Hattie (*Visible Learning*, 2008) and others has shown that to support learners' progress, it is important to encourage them to work toward crystal clear goals and to give them feedback that shows them what they are doing well and ways they are progressing, as well as letting them know next steps. This is especially true when the feedback is part of a whole system of learning that includes learners working toward goals that are ambitious and yet within grasp.

The bottom line conditions for effective writing instruction are, then:

- Writing needs to be taught like any other basic skill, with explicit instruction and ample opportunity for practice.
- Children deserve to write for real purposes, to write the kinds of texts that they see in the world and to write for an audience of readers.
- Writers write to put meaning onto the page. Children invest themselves in their writing when they choose topics that are important to them.
- Children deserve to be explicitly taught how to write.
- Children deserve the opportunity and instruction to cycle through the writing process.
- To write well, children need opportunities to read and to hear texts read, and to read as writers.
- Children need clear goals and frequent feedback.

Chapter 4

Upper-Elementary-Grade Writers and the Writing Process

WHEN I WAS A FOURTH-GRADER, my teacher taught writing by assigning us topics and telling us the expected page length. We wrote at home, bringing our completed essays, reports, summaries, and stories to school a few days after they were assigned. After a bit, we received the papers back, each with a grade for content, a grade for mechanics, and a few marginal comments. I expect many of us were "taught" writing that way. That was before the Writing Revolution.

A THUMBNAIL HISTORY OF WRITING PROCESS INSTRUCTION

Approximately three decades ago, a flurry of books and articles called for a writing revolution. Peter Elbow, Donald Murray, James Moffett, Ken Macrorie, and a series of edited volumes titled *Writers at Work* combined to popularize the message that when writers write, they do not sit down with a quill pen and immediately produce graceful, compelling prose. Instead, writers work through *a process of writing*, a process that contains recursive stages.

Different people use different terms when describing those stages. For example, some use the term *prewriting* and others *rehearsal*, but either way, widespread agreement has emerged that writers spend time preparing for writing. This stage involves living a "writerly life": collecting material for writing, weighing alternative plans for how a piece of writing might go, talking about one's topic, and reading texts that resemble the text one hopes to write. Rehearsal can also involve research.

Writers also *draft*. Early drafts are like playing in clay more than inscribing in marble; a writer might try alternative leads, explore different voices for a text, or freewrite, keeping her eyes glued on the subject and trying to capture the contours of it in tentative form. Writers shift back and forth between drafting and revising. *Revision* means, quite literally, "to see again." During revision, a writer pulls back from a draft to reread and rethink,

What is it I really want to say? What structure might best bring readers along to (and through) my content? Writers revise to discover and convey meaning and to use everything at their disposal to make that reading clear and potent to readers. Revision may involve rewriting an introduction, reconsidering the validity of one's evidence, and elaborating on important sections while deleting unimportant ones. Revision usually involves anticipating a reader's response. A writer may ask, What do I want my readers to think early on when they begin reading? Later? What do I want them to feel and do in response? Revision usually involves at least a second and often a third draft, since revisions that are bound by the contours of a first draft are held to the original structure, pace, and voice.

Finally, writers *edit*, which involves smoothing out, linking, tightening clarifying, fact checking, and correcting. During editing, writers think about spelling, punctuation, and word choice, yes, but writers also think about fact checking, language, and clarity. All of that sounds like a very long and arduous process, but there are times when a text is written quickly—say, in an hour or in half an hour. Even when writing quickly, writers still tend to go through abbreviated versions of each of these steps of the writing process.

The news that professional writers go through a process of writing was accompanied by the equally important news that even young children could experience the writing process. Three decades ago, a team of us from the University of New Hampshire—Donald Graves, Susan Sowers, and I, followed by many others—wrote articles and books showing that kindergartners and first-graders could rehearse, draft, revise, and edit their writing. The National Institute of Education study that Graves, Sowers, and I conducted helped the world realize that when teachers invite youngsters to write like the pros write and then observe and coach them in their process of writing as well as responding to their products, their growth in writing could be spectacular. The research on young children and the writing process was the talk of the town back in the eighties.

Since then, the idea that educators need to teach the writing process is so widely accepted that it's nearly a mainstream premise. Many standardized tests even include planning pages and remind writers to leave time to plan, revise, and edit their essays. Most language arts textbooks have incorporated the terms (if not the true concepts) of the writing process into their curriculum. And the Common Core State Standards leave no doubt but that all students are expected to develop facility in the process of writing. Anchor

standard 5 for writing reads, "Develop and strengthen writing as needed by planning, revising, editing, rewriting, or trying a new approach," and anchor standard 10 for writing reads, "Write routinely over extended time frames (time for research, reflection, and revision) and shorter time frames (a single sitting or a day or two) for a range of tasks, purposes, and audiences." More than this, the written products included in the appendix as benchmarks for student writing signal to any knowledgeable teacher that for students to meet the ambitious standards of the Common Core, they need to be explicitly taught the skills, strategies, and qualities of good writing.

AN OVERVIEW OF INSTRUCTIONAL APPROACHES TO THE WRITING PROCESS

Although the rhetoric behind the idea of teaching the writing process involves talk like this—"Children should be invited to write like real writers"—the truth is that children can only approximate the processes that adult writers use. An eight-year-old will not write exactly like Thomas Friedman, Robert Frost, or Patricia Polacco, nor do all adult writers write exactly like one another! Teachers who adopt a writing process approach to teaching writing are still left with the job of thinking through what the writing process will be that they plan to teach their students and how they will go about teaching that process.

I see teachers usually choosing one of these three possible approaches to teaching writing process:

- The "free to be me" approach
- The "assigned task" approach
- The "demonstrate, scaffold, release to write" approach

Here, I'll outline the assumptions underlying each of these approaches, before moving on to a detailed look at our approach, teaching units of study in a writing workshop, modeled on the third approach.

The Free to Be Me Approach

Following the free to be me approach, some teachers encourage each child to find his or her own individual writing process. On any one day in these classrooms, one child will write introductions to an information book, another will write a fiction story, and yet another will write several poems. In these classrooms, children cycle through the writing process in their own way and at their own pace. In a month, one child in a class may have written one very long rough draft, another will have worked two pieces through a series of revisions, and still another will have produced a dozen lightly revised texts. Teachers in these classrooms also place a priority on each child choosing his or her genre and topic. The teachers, meanwhile, look for teachable moments in which they can extend what children do as writers.

The underlying belief system of this approach is that the ability to write is somehow natural to all of us, within our DNA, and that under the right conditions, children will come to writing on their own, with little or no explicit instruction. This is neither my belief, nor am I a proponent of this approach.

The Assigned Tasks Approach

At the opposite extreme, there are teachers who teach writing by assigning writing. Often in these classrooms, the curriculum is a series of tasks that are replicas of (or sometimes interim steps toward) the task students will see on assessments. It is not unusual for the students to be prompted to write about a text the teacher has selected and the whole class has studied together, and often the teacher will have helped the class gather some of the ideas and information that will later become the content of the work students produce in response to assigned tasks. Each student, then, is assigned to write a paper of the same format, about the same text, using the same ideas the class has decided on together.

The tasks may be sequenced so that later tasks are more challenging than earlier tasks, so that they can be assembled into a larger project. For example, students might first be told to "write a paragraph describing character A, from text number 1. Be sure to give evidence by drawing on three examples from the text." Next, students might be assigned to "write an essay comparing and contrasting character A from text number 1 with character B from text number 2. Be sure you address at least three similarities and three differences and make references to both texts."

Rather than teaching replicable *ways* writers plan, structure, sequence, or revise their writing, teachers specify that students are to do these things. The tasks might include details such as: "Show your planning work. Write

with a thesis and three supporting paragraphs. Your work should be written in complete sentences with correct punctuation." The assumption is that assigning the writing process is a sufficient enough way to teach it. If there is feedback given, it usually involves an assessment as to whether students fulfilled expectations. The feedback is task-specific and not intended to transfer to other pieces of writing. Again, as is probably clear, this approach is not one I endorse.

The Demonstrate, Scaffold, Release to Write Approach

My colleagues and I fall into a third category—as do many others who care about the teaching of the writing process. Our goal is to actively and explicitly teach students how to draw on a repertoire of skills and strategies that have served accomplished writers well over the years. We look for evidence that students have the knowledge, skills, and habits to draw on these planning, drafting, revision, and editing skills whether they are working on extended writing projects or on a flash-draft. To help students develop the repertoire of skills for each stage of the writing process, we *demonstrate* the process that writers often use to do the type of writing being studied, and we *scaffold* students to practice the steps of the process, so that when we *release* them to write without support, they are able to independently draw on a repertoire of strategies we've taught. As students continue to write with less scaffolding, we teach by using assessments and goals, feedback, and guided practice.

A RATIONALE FOR CHOOSING THE THIRD APPROACH AND A DESCRIPTION OF HOW THIS TRANSLATES INTO UNITS OF STUDY FOR A WRITING WORKSHOP

To understand what this third approach—our approach—to teaching writing involves, consider this metaphor. Think, for a moment, about the way a ski instructor travels down a mountain with a class of students. We argue that when students travel roughly in sync through steps in the writing process, it provides extra teaching opportunities that are not unlike the sort a ski instructor finds at intervals down the mountain. If the instructor says, "See those hay bales alongside that pole? Let's stop there. Before you get to those bales, work on . . ." Then the young skiers receive some demonstration teaching and lots of pointers. After skiing to the interim spot of the hay bales, there is time for assessment and another "See that rise, where that cluster of skiers have stopped to look at the view? Let's stop there. This time, work on . . ." This sort of instruction allows a teacher to do a lot of explicit teaching.

As long as the process you teach rings true—that is, a process that real writers might actually participate in—and as long as students are invested in their writing and you are teaching strategies that help them write well beyond this piece, this sort of synchronized progression through the writing process seems to us to be warranted. It also supports the CCSS writing anchor standard 10: "Write routinely over extended time frames (time for research, reflection and revision) . . . for a range of tasks, purposes, and audiences."

So now let's imagine that we want to teach opinion writing to third-graders. We'd want all students to be working in sync with one another for the first part of the unit, so we'd need to decide on a sequence of shared tasks. Perhaps we'd first ask students to do some quick work on writing persuasive letters, using that work to remind them of what they'd learned in previous years. Then we'd engage them in a longer effort to write editorials. The unit would involve a sequence of tasks, not assignment-based but instead writing process-based and therefore transferable to children's work beyond the task at hand.

Meanwhile, we'd teach students a growing repertoire of strategies for each step of the opinion writing process. For example, students first would need to develop and draw on a number of ways to choose their topics, so we'd teach them strategies for generating topics. The first strategies are especially accessible ones—writers might jot issues around which they have strong opinions.

By the time students are writing editorials, they could draw on this early strategy, or some others including taking an "issues walk" wherein they walk through a place—say, the school playground at recess or the school cafeteria at lunch—noticing issues they could address. Alternatively, they take an "issues walk" through the daily newspaper.

Of course, students will, by now, have not only generated topics and claims about those topics, but they will also have gone on to write a whole sequence

of opinion pieces. And while they were doing that writing, we will have also helped them develop a repertoire of planning techniques, starting with a simple one (listing research across their fingers) and progressing to a more complicated way of planning. All these ways of planning, like the ways of generating topics, will cumulate on charts and be drawn on repeatedly. Of course, after students have planned and before they flash-draft an entire piece, there will be more instruction.

But, as in life, one will not always ski with an instructor at one's side, setting goals, assessing, and planning. So it is also important for instruction to happen in less frequent intervals that are designed to give learners time to assume some of the instructor's role. The instructor might say, "This time, will you and a peer ski together and stop at the same places where we stopped, only this time, will the two of you reflect on how the last bit went and give each other some tips to keep in mind as you ski the next interval?" Then again, the instructor might say, "This lesson is about to end, but why don't you take a few more runs? Let's review the things you need to work on. And listen—make the first run on a green-circle trail, and only move up to the blues if you feel comfortable on that first trail." It is in just that way that teachers of writing teach—working with a sequence of tasks, and explicitly teaching strategies and skills but also removing scaffolds as quickly as possible to give students longer chunks of time within which to do their *own* work.

It is important to point out that writers need to be able to plan, draft, revise, and edit while producing work for fast-approaching deadlines, so the process that I've just described can also be accelerated, with rehearsal occurring in the mind's eye, with revision happening during rehearsal. Instruction needs to support both the more extended and the more abbreviated writing processes so that students learn that these are variations of each other. That is, even when a writer must produce a text within an hour, the proficient writer can still call on an intense, if abbreviated, version of the writing process.

As a unit of study unrolls (and also as the year unrolls and as one year follows the next), students work on more challenging tasks and with more independence. Perhaps after students have progressed in sync through one or two cycles of opinion writing, doing the work we described to produce persuasive letters and editorials, the teacher might alert the class to a real issue that has arisen in the community and suggest that students choose the form of persuasive writing they most want to use to address that issue, angling their writing to the audience they want to address, and writing quickly—perhaps over the space of just two days—transferring all they have learned previously to their effort to address a timely issue in their community.

In the demonstrate, scaffold, release approach, how does one calibrate the challenge level of instruction?

Of course, as the ski instruction continues, the student progresses from blue-circle trails to black diamond trails. In the same way, the writing work that students tackle becomes progressively more challenging.

For example, toward the start of a school year, when working with children who are new to the writing process, you might teach a unit in which students write information texts on topics of personal expertise. Within that unit, you will presumably teach your students to think about the logical structure of their topic and to use the table of contents as a way to structure the draft. Two months later, you might begin yet another information writing unit, this one on writing research reports. When coaching students to progress through the writing process on their research reports, you will remind them of strategies they used earlier when writing information texts on topics of personal expertise. "Do you remember how you thought about the component parts of your topic and made a table of contents? Well, you will want to do that again for this new topic, but this time you need to check your sources to be sure that the subtopics you imagine addressing are ones on which you can find adequate information." Students will probably still be encouraged to work with the structure of their texts in very concrete ways by drafting and revising their tables of contents, but you may keep in mind that your very strongest students could be graduated from that reliance on a table of contents. It is far more challenging to use transitions not only within a section of a text but also between those sections. When writers forego a table of contents and try to stitch together the chunks of an extended piece of writing, they often need help learning about A heads, B heads, and C heads and certainly need to learn to use a hierarchy of transition phrases within an extended text. My

point is, however, that teaching writing involves rallying students to tackle a progression of writing challenges.

THE DISTINCTIVE CHARACTERISTICS OF UPPER-ELEMENTARY STUDENTS' WRITING PROCESS

Of course, concomitant with deciding on the approach you will use with your students and with thinking through the ways this approach will allow you to differentiate your teaching based on your particular students' needs, you also need to consider the age of your students and the volume and pace of work you can expect of them, as well as what materials—paper—you need to provide for them to be successful. As I outline next, these expectations vary across the grades, and you'll want to be sure you not only provide the writing tools to set your students up for success, but that you also set high—but achievable—goals for the amount of writing your students do in a day, a week, a month, and for the speed at which they will move through the writing process.

How is the writing process of a fifth-grader apt to differ from that of a second-grader?

Stamina and Pacing across the Grades

As children become older and more experienced, they are able to write fluently and quickly. By the time a child is in fifth grade, the youngster should be able to produce a quick and competent flash-draft—perhaps a page and a half or two pages in length—within half an hour or forty-five minutes. If pressed to do so, such a youngster can speed through the process of deliberation over the focus and structure of a text to simply pick up the pen and write. For such a student, writing a flash-draft is a relatively easy process.

It is perhaps more significant to say, however, that by the time a child is in fifth grade, he or she can use extended time to plan strategically for work on a piece of writing. Such a writer will plan not only the content to include but also the challenges that need to be met and the strategies that need to be employed. Such a writer could work productively on a single piece of writing over a sequence of weeks, shifting from planning to drafting, to assessing and revising, and then, to planning and drafting again. That is, a fifth-grader who has grown up in a writing workshop has enough rehearsal and revision strategies in his or her repertoire, and enough ability and skill at self-assessment and knowledge of good writing, that the youngster can, with coaching and feedback, sustain work on a piece of writing for a long stretch of time.

One of the important things to realize when thinking about how writing processes develop over time is that a more pressing deadline and briefer writing process can mean that the challenge level of the task has increased, or it can mean that the challenge level has decreased, depending on the amount of deliberate, strategic thinking that the writer incorporates into his or her process. Producing an entire piece of writing within a more focused span of time can lower the challenge level of the work if this leads a writer to forgo deliberation and strategic work.

When thinking about how the writing process of a second-grader differs from that of a fifth-grader, then, it is important to note that second-graders are not apt to have the capacity to sustain work on a single text for very long. It may seem counterintuitive to suggest that younger children write more quickly than older students, but bear in mind that early in the year, kindergarten children write ten pieces a day! Five-year-olds pick up a marker pen, make a scrawl in the middle of a blank page, declare themselves done, and move to the next page. For these children it is a mark of progress when they learn that writers first think of what they want to say and only then put what is in their mind onto the page (in this instance, through a representational picture). It is yet another step ahead for young writers to later learn they can return to the picture once more to add details, even accompanying labels, and to make another page that shows what happened next. At least at the start of the year, first-graders tend to write a new piece every day or two. Second-graders average closer to three days on a piece, with the more experienced writers tackling an ambitious enough project that the process is longer and more involved. So don't think that there is something inherently advanced about writing an entire text in one day and then revising and editing it the next day!

In third grade, children can, with your support, work a bit longer and more deeply on some pieces of writing. Whereas second-graders tend to take

up a blank booklet, think about a topic, perhaps story-tell or teach someone this topic, then write a draft perhaps over the course of two days, then revise the draft with spider legs or flaps for inserts, third-graders can do more work at each stage of the process. Prior to settling on a topic, third-graders might fast-draft a bunch of quick stories or story blurbs or opinion entries. If they receive instruction, they can ratchet up the level of those fast-drafts, getting some important lessons into their bones very early on in the unit (and in the process). Then they can choose one topic and piece of writing to develop.

Once a third-grade writer knows his or her topic and general content and is trying to write really well about that topic, it is time for some intense, quick research of an exemplar text, followed by drafting. We hope third-graders write the bulk of a draft in a single day, writing fast and furiously. If their text sprawls across a number of days, it generally becomes less cohesive. Of course, by fifth grade rehearsal can be a much more involved process. Any work that students did once through revision can later become part of rehearsal. If third-graders once revise opinion writing to make sure their reasons are equally valid, another time when they are writing an opinion piece, they can review a proposed plan for their writing and question the relative strength of their reasons.

Revision across the Grades

Between kindergarten and fifth grade, children's abilities to revise become more sophisticated. Kindergartners revise on the first day of school, but those earliest revisions typically only involve adding more details onto their drawings. In time, kindergartners will add more pages to a story and more labels or sentences to a page. By first and second grade (although with some students this happens at the end of kindergarten) children will tape flaps onto the edges of a draft and use those flaps to insert details and direct quotes and elaborating information. They will sometimes write new leads or endings, taping them on top of the earlier versions. They may even resequence pages. They will certainly rewrite key pages to include more detail; show, not tell, their feelings; answer readers' questions; and so forth.

Revision for upper-elementary students begins much earlier in the writing process. As should be clear from my discussion of rehearsal strategies, if children have grown up participating in writing workshops, by the time they are in third grade, revision will actually begin when they draft a timeline or an outline and use these graphic organizers to help them anticipate difficulties and then to imagine new possibilities for the upcoming draft. Similarly, when upper-elementary students draft and revise leads, they eventually do so not only with an eye toward a good lead but also with recognition that each lead represents a different way the text could go: "If I start it this way, it'll take too long to get to the main part." By fifth grade, children begin to grasp that the process of writing a thesis statement is actually the process of writing an essay, in miniature.

So, if you teach third-graders, you will sometimes want them to ski the mountain quickly and sometimes slowly. Slow for a third-grader won't be as slow as what you can expect of a fifth-grader. When a third-grader prolongs work on a single text, taking time to work hard to vary the kinds of elaboration he or she uses, to include examples and discuss them, for example, that work will probably span a week or a week and a half of writing workshops—not more. Revision might last a few days.

On the other hand, although your fifth-graders will also sometimes write flash-drafts or cycle through the entire writing process in a few days (or even in a day), these students can also work for longer stretches of time. The biggest difference between third and fifth grade involves the scale of revision work, with fifth-graders often writing multiple drafts and often shifting between writing and studying a mentor text or writing and research in the midst of writing. Fifth-graders, too, are apt to work on texts that are considerably longer than those written by third-graders. A typical personal narrative for a fifth-grader will probably be two and a half pages, a typical fiction story, twice that length, and a research paper is apt to be more than five pages, but written in chapters.

How does the writing paper used by writers in grades 3–5 differ from that used by K–2 writers?

Booklets

It is important for children of all ages to write on paper that physically embodies the expectations for their writing process and for the particular genre in which they are writing. In K–2 classrooms, children do most of their writing in small booklets, with each page carrying a space for drawing before writing—varying the expectations for the ratio of drawing to writing—and with each page carrying also either the next subtopic or the next step in the larger text. That is, the turn of the page functions almost like paragraphs.

Many teachers find it helpful to start the third-grade year by providing youngsters with a grown-up version of a K–2 booklet. Although third-graders' booklets do not generally contain spaces for drawing, the children can use subheadings (in every genre) to mark the focus of a particular page. In a persuasive speech, for example, one page might be titled "Introduction," and others "The Reasons," "How We Should Recycle," "What If We Don't?," and "Conclusion." Each of those pages would probably contain just a paragraph, but the turn of the page and the presence of subheads could help some third-graders chunk their texts. By the time children are in fifth grade, it will be less important for the paper on which they write to physically support chunking and elaboration. These children should be able to use paragraphs, generalizations/topic sentences, and transitions to accomplish similar jobs.

Notebooks

Most upper-grade writing workshop teachers find that if students keep writer's notebooks and use those notebooks as a workbench—as a place to do the work involved in the stages of their writing process—then it helps the students become invested in developing processes and strategies as writers. First promulgated by Donald Murray, the Pulitzer prize–winning author of *A Writer Teaches Writing* and a score of other books on writing instruction and journalism coach to *The Boston Globe* and the Pointer Institute, writer's notebooks have come to represent a writing process approach to teaching writing. Murray, who calls these tools *daybooks*, especially emphasizes the importance of writing often so as to "not walk around unwritten." When a person lives with a writer's notebook at his or her side, this more likely leads that person to put insights, observations, quotes, and anecdotes onto the page long before the writer has chosen a topic or begun work toward a specific writing project. Murray found that when an observation, a response to a book, an account of an experience, and some questions, for example, are laid side by side on the page, out of that mix, ideas for writing grow. "I compost my life," he says in describing "the great garage sale of junk" from which his new insights and ideas developed.

I wrote a book in the early 1990s, *Living Between the Lines*, that especially embraces Murray's definition of writer's notebooks as the rich compost kept by a wide-awake writer. I reread that book now and feel a wave of nostalgia for an era when writing instruction in schools emphasized living the writerly life, encouraging students to pause to savor the wake of wonder left by a cicada bug. I feel enormous fondness for the image of notebooks as a "great garage sale" of entries. I hope some of the spirit of that early way of bringing the writing process into classrooms remains in this series.

You'll see us telling students that writers collect small stories in their notebooks and reread their notebooks to decide which of those stories they want to develop into major pieces of writing. You will see us suggest that writers can jot possible leads in a notebook or plan alternate structures for a text. You'll see the notebooks change as writers progress from working on narrative writing to working on essay writing. Now we'll say, "Writers don't only collect small stories. Writers also collect big ideas." During these times when we talk about the writer's notebook, there will be lots of references to our own notebooks and to the notebooks kept by published writers. Although notebooks will predominate during rehearsal in particular, youngsters leave those notebooks behind when they go to write draft one, which will be written on one side of lined paper, outside the notebook, so that the draft can be scissored apart or can have flaps added to the margins during revision. But even when students are drafting on lined paper, outside the notebook, they may return to the notebook as a craftsperson returns to the workbench, to hammer out a possible ending or to refine a particular part.

But times have changed, and my colleagues and I talk about writer's notebooks differently and, frankly, a bit less than we once did. We still rally students in grades 3–8 to keep writer's notebooks, and we use the presence of writer's notebooks as a physical embodiment of the writerly life. And we still talk about the importance of living with wide-awake attentiveness. But one of the most important sections of a writer's notebook is a section we didn't even consider years ago, and that's the final section where writers keep track of their goals, their progress toward their goals, and their conferences.

Our emphasis on writer's notebooks has also changed because increasingly, we spend time emphasizing the role of research and the importance of structuring a text and writing within genre-specific specifications. When students are writing expository texts, where one page does not necessarily follow the next, where information needs to be sorted, chunked, and resorted, the binding of a notebook can be restrictive. If writers are researching the American Revolution and want to sort their notes to imagine perhaps writing a compare-and-contrast essay, this is not as easy to do if the notes are bound into a notebook.

You will see, then, that in this series, we start each year with a big emphasis on writer's notebooks and on the importance of living the writerly life. We try to give continued attention to the tool of writer's notebooks throughout all the units and all the years, but the truth is that they play a less dominant role as writers work in some units that require a special amount of sorting and categorizing of information. In those units, you will see that some teachers replace notebooks with booklets comprised of four to seven pages of notebook paper, stapled together, on which writers write on one side only. Booklets function as temporary notebooks, as notebooks that can be scissored apart. They allow writers to keep their notes, jottings, and plans in one place for a time, but they are also made to be disassembled and reassembled into a rough outline for a draft or, in some instances, into pieces of a draft.

You will find other suggestions for ways materials can support the writing process, and you'll discover these suggestions as you proceed through the curriculum itself. For now, it is important to know that one of the ways to scaffold a young person's writing process is to provide materials that do some of this work. It is important to know, too, that if you grew up on my earlier books and find yourself wondering, How does the approach supported in Units of Study in Opinion, Information, and Narrative Writing align with the approach described in *Living Between the Lines*? (or in books such as Anne LaMott's *Bird by Bird* or Katie Wood Ray's *Wondrous Words*), your question is astute.

> *"A writer's notebook leads a person to put insights, observations, quotes, and anecdotes onto the page long before the writer has chosen a topic."*

As the world looks for instruction to emphasize expository writing more than narrative, structure more than detail, research more than mining personal experience, visible, accountable progress more than deeply personal investment, a sequence of tasks over an investment in authentic processes, our focus on writer's notebooks has decreased a bit, with more attention focused on writing files and booklets, portfolios, and self-assessment.

I say this to help you understand the field of writing and the history of approaches to teaching writing. I think transparency is helpful because if you understand the trail on which our thinking has taken us, you can choose to follow that trail or deviate from it. I'd be proud as punch if some of you mull over what I've written here and decide that for you, notebooks represent a more authentic, organic version of the writing process and that you'll find ways to make them more predominant in your teaching than they are in these units. My nephew is a new teacher, just learning to teach the writing process. I'd be happy as a clam if Peter was to come to me and say, "I've been reading over your earlier books and Don Murray's work, and books by writers for writers, too, and I think I'm going to make a bigger deal of writer's notebooks than you do in this series. I think I will keep students writing in notebooks—not in folders or booklets— even if that means Xeroxing their entries when they need to spread things out in front of them to categorize." I'd say, "Great. I can definitely see why you'd do that." Then again, if Peter was to say, "I've been thinking about this topic really seriously, and I think that for my third-graders, I'd rather staple together a unit-specific notebook than channel them to buy a big bound notebook at Staples, because for now I think I want to make lined paper with fewer lines for the strugglers, borrowing some ideas from second-grade teachers, and in general, I'd rather they have the experience of filling up one notebook after another than writing, writing, writing in an endless notebook," I'd also say, "Great."

This is an area in which you'll make some decisions, knowing that either way, I have your back.

A MORE DETAILED LOOK AT THE WRITING PROCESS FOR WRITERS, GRADES 3–5

Now that you have an understanding of some of the reasons and rationales for decisions we've made in this series and have a road map for deciding on the materials you'll want to supply your students with as they begin living writerly lives, let's look more closely at the writing process you and your students will go through—many times—in different units and genres and at various pacing.

Rehearsal for Writing

The first stage of the writing process may be called *rehearsal* or *prewriting* or *gathering entries*. Children who have grown up in writing workshops during the primary grades will enter third or fourth grade able to generate ideas for writing. When asked to choose topics for writing, children who do not have a lot of writing experience, however, may sit in front of blank pages saying, "I don't have anything that I know about" or "I don't have strong opinions on anything" or "Nothing interesting happens in my life." In these instances, helping children rehearse for writing means helping them learn strategies for generating content and learn, too, that their ideas, knowledge, and experiences *are* worth writing about. But rehearsal is never just about generating content. It also involves planning the process and structure of a piece.

The process varies by genre and focus.

The strategies for generating ideas for writing will be somewhat different depending on whether a student is writing a literary essay, an editorial, a story, a research report, and so on. For example, when teaching students to write literary essays, I might teach them that it sometimes helps to read with a set of questions in mind: What is this text *really* about? What line or passage in this text captures what the author is mostly trying to convey? Then again, I might let them know that a literary essayist can annotate the text, marking parts that especially stand out and then revisit those parts to ask, Why did this stand out for me?

On the other hand, when students write personal narrative entries, I might suggest they take a minute to think of a person (or place or thing) that matters to them and then list several times when they did something with that person (or in that place or with that thing). Then I would suggest they reread that list, select one episode that they remember with crystal clarity and that holds some significance, and begin to write the story of that one episode.

The important thing is that once youngsters have been taught a few strategies, they will begin developing a repertoire of genre-specific strategies for generating writing, and they can learn to draw on that repertoire to generate their own writing topics. They can also draw on that repertoire to generate more focused topics even when assigned a general one. That is, a researcher writing on Westward Expansion still needs to generate his or her angled topic and can use the repertoire of generating strategies to do so. More than this, young people can learn that when they live as writers, the details of their lives and their thinking are worth developing. They learn to live (experiencing, observing, listening, reading) with a writer's consciousness, thinking, I should write about this.

A big part of rehearsal involves generating ideas for writing.

Many people think of rehearsal as a time for writers to plan a draft before embarking on it, and it is true that planning is central to rehearsal. But especially when writers write often and are given responsibility for generating topics for their writing, a big part of rehearsal involves gathering ideas for writing.

Earlier, when discussing the use of writer's notebooks, I talked about the importance of teaching students to live writerly lives. If a person writes often, then rehearsal is not just a discrete activity one does at the desk just before embarking on a draft. It is also a sort of wide-awake way of living. When asked about the way that writing can alter a person's perception of his or her life, Katherine Paterson, the author of *Bridge to Terabithia*, told the story of her son David calling to her to come watch as a cicada shed its skin. As they crouched alongside the bug, they watched a tiny slit appear on the bug's back; as it was gradually pulled down as if the bug had a waist-length zipper, they saw a hint of colors through the slit. Then there were more colors—aqua, yellow, green, cream, flecks of gold like jewelry on its head. Then the wings emerged, crumpled ribbons at first, then stretched out. As they watched, the cicada swung like an acrobat onto a new twig and then flew off, "oblivious to the wake of wonder it left behind." Paterson said, "As I let that wake of wonder wash over me, I realized that this was the real gift I want to give children, for what good are straight teeth and trumpet lessons to a person who cannot see the grandeur that the world is charged with?" (*Gates of Excellence: On Reading and Writing Books for Children*, 1981, 20).

Writer's notebooks support the consciousness Paterson believes is so critical to writing. When young people (and their teachers) carry notebooks (literally and figuratively) through their lives, this supports them in living with the perspective of being a writer, seeing potential stories, essays, and editorials everywhere. Writers notice something and think, I should jot this down. I may want to make something of it. In time, students come to the writing workshop already knowing what they want to write, which suggests that they see potential stories and essays everywhere and also are able to select, from all the possibilities, ideas that seem to them to be worth developing and planning as a first draft.

This alertness to potential topics is absolutely essential to any writer who mines his or her life for potential writing topics, but it is also part of the process for writers who write about their research and reading. For example, once I had decided to write a book about the Common Core State Standards, you can be sure that I went through life living as a magnet on that topic. Anything that I read or heard or saw relating to that topic became grist for my writing mill. I knew that I needed to develop my own insights about and analysis of the CCSS, so I collected observations, recorded patterns, jotted down questions, and used this "great garage sale" of related junk to spark ideas and insights. As part of my rehearsal, I read over everything I had gathered and jotted insights such as "A surprising number of people regard papers such as 'A Publisher's Guide to the CCSS' or 'The Seven Shifts'—papers that reflect one organization's interpretation of the Common Core State Standards—as what the Common Core State Standards actually say. If people would only go back to the actual source, they'd realize that the CCSS and those documents differ in dramatic ways." Some insights I jotted ended up becoming central ideas, in which case I then gathered more facts to support that insight—again, living a writerly life, only this time with a more focused magnetic force. In the same way, a student researching the American Revolution will first collect insights and ideas related to that broad writing territory, and then when a more focused topic emerges, she will collect sources around that narrowed topic.

Rehearsal also involves weighing possible structures.

Of course, rehearsal for writing also involves imagining possible structures for a piece of writing and thinking about how one's content could fit into one structure, another, and another. "In my report on the Boston Tea Party, do I have enough information about the chronology of the event to write a chapter on the start of it, the middle of it, the ending of it, and the aftereffect? What if I lump together the ending and the aftereffect? Could I write about different subtopics instead? If so, what would they be? If I tried to write a subsection on the causes, do I have that information? What about a subsection on the people involved?"

As students work on their leads, their introductions, and their thesis statements, they try on different ways that their texts might go. You can teach writers that planning can involve drafting and revising leads or introductions or thesis statements. For example, I recommend that children who are writing narratives try writing a lead by mentally replaying the event and then capturing the initial actions or dialogue on the page, because writing a lead in this fashion helps writers envision and dramatize the unfolding story in ways that allow readers to experience that story. If a narrative writer decides that an orienting statement is needed at the very start of a story, I recommend he add that later. I recommend that information writers learn, eventually, to think of themselves as tour guides, taking readers on a tour of their topic, and to learn that an overview up front helps readers anticipate where the tour will lead. Of course, at first students will draft and revise alternative leads or introductions without realizing that in doing so, they are exploring alternative ways their entire texts might go.

With experience, everything students do one time during revision can move forward, becoming part of rehearsal.

As children become more experienced and skilled as writers, everything they learn through revision can move forward into the rehearsal stage of their writing. For example, some writers begin the year writing about gigantic topics—"My trip to my grandma's house." Only during revision do these children reread their writing and think, Which *particular aspect* of my visit do I want to address? With experience, however, these same children will soon learn to generate focused ideas for writing and to screen those ideas, asking, Will this story (essay, editorial, report) be focused enough?

Similarly, the initial entries children write will not be detailed, nor will they be written in paragraphs, and so forth. As children learn more and more, however, the work they do during rehearsal will incorporate features they earlier learned only through revision. These might include writing with details and paragraphing but may also include showing rather than telling, developing the heart of the story, including text citations, deliberately varying the kinds of supportive evidence used, or any one of a host of other skills. In other words,

the more skilled and experienced a writer becomes, the more that writer can do during rehearsal.

Experienced writers are apt to do more—and spend longer—in rehearsal.

A professional writer might delay drafting for six months to a year, using this time to write and critique a whole sequence of different plans for a text! Such a writer would prefer progressing through multiple *outlines* rather than multiple *drafts*. A nine-year-old child, of course, will not find it easy to scrawl a few words onto the page and then look at this outline or plan, imagining from the abbreviated notes the larger text or the problems such a text might engender—let alone imagining another way that the text could have been written. Still, nine-year-olds can live like writers, seeing potential for stories, arguments, and essays everywhere. They can use all they know about good writing (or good narratives, good essays, and so on) to lift the level of their entries, thus giving them taller shoulders on which to stand when they select one entry to develop into a major piece of writing. These children can also learn to talk through the writing they plan to do, trying out one way and then another of approaching their subjects, observing their audiences' responses to those "in-the-air" drafts, and revising the drafts before they've even written a word.

And certainly, upper-elementary students can learn to make simple outlines, revising these in preparation for writing. They can look at a rough diagram of an editorial and think, My last reason is sort of the same as the second one. I should make them more distinct from one another. They can realize the supporting information in their research report is not varied and set out to gather a wider variety. Then, too, they can look at a story mountain and think, I need to really build up this part of my story. It is my rising action. I need to show how he tried, tried, tried. All of this can be done in preparation for writing a draft.

Drafting

While rehearsal and revision both involve the deliberate use of one strategy or another, drafting is less strategic. After all the work of collecting, choosing, planning, teaching others, storytelling, and imagining the piece laid out on the page, the writer takes pen in hand and writes.

For many writers, velocity is important when drafting. William Stafford describes writing this way: "When I write . . . I get pen and paper, take a glance out the window (often it is dark out there), and wait. It is like fishing. But I do not wait long, for there is always a nibble—and this is where receptivity comes in. To get started, I will accept anything that occurs to me. Something always occurs . . . If I put down something, that thing will help the next thing come, and I'm off. If I let the process go on, things will occur to me that were not at all in my mind when I started . . . For the person who follows with trust and forgiveness what occurs to him, the world remains always ready and deep, an inexhaustible environment" ("A Way of Writing" in *To Compose: Teaching Writing in High School and College*, 1990, 17–20).

When writing "fast and furious" or "strong and long," writers need to be positioned in ways that pay off for them. For a narrative writer, for example, it is helpful if the writer has made what I refer to as a "movie in the mind" and keeps her eye on that movie. Peter Elbow, the great writing teacher and author of *Writing with Power*, advises, "Don't *describe* the tree. *See* the tree!" He is not really saying anything different than I am when I suggest that writers make a movie in their mind and keep their eyes on that movie.

The larger point is actually not even about narrative writing. It is that powerful writing comes not from thinking about penmanship, word choice, complex sentences, and showing, not telling, as one writes. Powerful writing comes from being full of one's subject and keeping one's eye on that subject.

The essayist doesn't make a movie in his or her mind, but instead assumes a teaching/explaining/persuading stance, feels full of his or her subject, and then when putting pen to page, tries to write in ways that teach or persuade readers, as if those readers were standing before the writer.

Either way, one hopes that writers write quickly, knowing that writing a draft is playing in clay, not inscribing in marble, and that there will be time another day to roll up one's sleeves and set to work. Writers are more willing to revise if the draft is written quickly—as a trial effort. Revision, then, becomes a time to see what the fast and furious writing yielded.

"As students become more experienced as writers, their revision can happen in their mind's eye."

Revision

Writing is a powerful tool for capturing thought precisely because when a person writes, putting whatever occurs to her on the page, the writer can put those initial thoughts away, in a pocket or file, and on another day she can take them out to reread and rethink.

Over time, writers learn to resee and reconsider first drafts through a variety of lenses. For starters, the writer pretends to be a stranger to these ideas, reading the draft as if encountering it for the first time, spying on her experience of the draft to imagine what a reader's experience of and reaction to it might be. Doing this, the writer is asking, What will a reader make of this? Are there sections that are unclear, claims that require more evidence? This sort of rereading can fuel powerful revisions.

Writers can also reread to consider a draft in light of the writer's goals, asking, Can I see the qualities of writing that I'm aiming to achieve in this text? In other words, if a writer has studied effective essays and learned that essays often shift between precise examples and overarching ideas, the writer might look at her own essay and ask, Does my essay shift between the general and the specific?

If a writer has studied a mentor text, noting qualities that work well in it, the writer can say, "Let me see if I've brought that quality into this draft" and might locate places in the text where he or she could try that same effect. In a similar way, if a writer learns about—or hears about—a technique that other writers have used to good effect, revision can be a time to try bringing that same technique into one's own draft. "E. B. White suggests the final sentence in a paragraph is the most important and should propel the reader forward," the writer might state. "I'm going to reread my final sentences and see if I can make them stronger."

Writers can, more generally, reread their own writing, asking, "What works here that I can build on?" and "What doesn't work here that I can repair or eliminate?"

As students become more experienced as writers, more of their revision can happen in their mind's eye as they weigh one alternative against another.

I find that at the start of third grade, not much productive revision work happens in the abstract. If a youngster is going to try alternative introductions, for example, it probably makes sense for the writer to literally write each alternative down on the page. Once children are in fifth grade, if they are experienced with the writing process, they will be able to do much more musing over questions and use graphic organizers, fragments of writing, and notes to pin tentative ideas on the page, weighing those ideas against others.

The most sophisticated and important sort of revision isn't fixing up one's text so that it works more effectively to convey one's meaning. Instead, the most sophisticated sorts of revisions involve the writer looking *through his draft to come to a deeper, more nuanced, more thoughtful understanding of his content*. This sort of revision begins with the writer asking, "What am I trying to say?" and then revising to highlight that meaning. In time, this sort of revision becomes more exploratory. Writers venture into unexplored terrain and stumble on new insights that illuminate a topic not only for the reader but also for the writer. When a writer anticipates that he or she will revise to discover and clarify what the text is really saying, such a writer eventually drafts differently. For such writers, it can sometimes work to write without knowing exactly what it is they want to say; then they turn around and read their writing and in doing so, think, What is it that I think? and What surprises me, astonishes me, makes me catch my breath?

Editing

Professional writers tend to postpone editing until the text is ready to be published. Like adult writers, children learn the value of writing rough drafts quickly, without pausing to use *Roget's Thesaurus* or even a dictionary in the midst of drafting. And like adult writers, children do not pore over a draft, worrying that every convention is correct, until it is time for the writing to be published.

Once the main structure and content of a draft has been revised so that the text now feels stable, writers begin to reread, checking each sentence, word, and letter from a "when you falter, alter" perspective. In your writing workshop, you will probably teach students to read each draft successive times, each time with a new lens. Among other things, the child will read for spelling. If the child senses that a word is misspelled, she circles that word and then tries it again in the margin. To do this, the youngster needs to look

at the approximate spelling, asking, "Is this partly right?" and then copy that part of the word. The child also needs to ask, "What other words do I know that might be spelled like this one?" and to use the words the child can spell to help spell unknown words. You will want to encourage your students to use resources to help them, including a dictionary and each other.

Editing, however, involves much more than correcting spelling, and you will want to teach students to check that they've included end punctuation, that their verb tenses agree, that they use a variety of punctuation and sentence structures, that their words are precise, and that their pronoun references are clear. "Does this sound right?" a writer asks. "Is this exactly true? Are the words precisely chosen? Will the punctuation give readers the road signs they need?"

You will teach editing within minilessons and also within mid-workshop teachings, share sessions, and homework assignments. Obviously, you will tailor your lessons so they are roughly aligned with what most of the class needs, using small-group instruction to provide special support for children who need it. As the year unfolds, youngsters will have access to a growing list of skills. In September, you may expect children to edit their writing looking for high-frequency words found on the class word wall, for end punctuation, and for paragraphing. By May, children will check that their pronoun references are clear and their sentence structures varied.

Once children have been taught to edit with particular concerns in mind, then those skills and strategies need to move forward in the writing process, becoming part of the writer's repertoire of skills that he draws on while scrawling a rough draft. So while you will not want your students to fret about writing perfectly correct drafts, it will also not be helpful for them to postpone all thought of spelling and punctuation until the final throes of working on a manuscript. Over time, you will want your students to be able to use roughly correct spelling and punctuation and paragraphing even when they write very fast rough drafts. As part of this, it will be important that they learn to spell a growing bank of words (and syllables) automatically. And punctuation cannot be an afterthought, inserted into a manuscript just before it goes to press! So you will channel your students to take a few minutes as they write their rough drafts to make sure that the conventions they "almost know" are under control. Then, during editing, you can encourage students to reexamine conventions that pose problems for them, relying on resources and one another to edit these problematic areas.

Once a child has edited her own writing, you will want to confer with the child, teaching the writer another few strategies she can use to edit the text. Perhaps the child will have added quotation marks correctly but will have not yet mastered the punctuation that accompanies quotations. In the editing conference, you can support that child's use of quotation marks and show the youngster the next step toward correct handling of quotations. In your editing conference, you might go over one quote with the student and then ask her to read through the draft, fixing other quotations in a similar way. Meanwhile, however, there will be some incorrect spellings and some problems with verb tenses, and you might choose not to tackle those. That is, in editing conferences, like in every other kind of conference, a teacher makes a choice, teaching the child a few things that seem to be within the child's reach.

Before the student's work is published, many teachers go through the final draft as a copy editor would, correcting it. The student then recopies the piece, correcting most (but rarely all) of the errors. This final step calls for a decision. If you correct the child's final work before children recopy it, then that text will be easier for others to read. On the other hand, if you do this, then the child's final work does not really reflect what the child can do independently, and it will be harder for you to hold yourself to being sure that children are growing in their abilities to correct their own writing. It is important, therefore, that the next-to-final draft is kept in the child's portfolio.

Cycling through the Entire Process

Just as children need to have a sense of how a narrative or an essay or an information text tends to go, they need to have a sense of how the process of writing that kind of text is apt to go. For example, you don't want the stage of gathering entries, doing research, or collecting reasons and evidence to be so long that children can't feel that it is just a prelude to selecting one seed idea or one thesis statement or one topic to develop. The gathering of entries and collecting of information can't feel like an end in itself—the stage of using those entries, research, and information has to follow directly on it, within a short enough time frame that kids recognize the reasons they collected those entries. I want children to plan and draft their writing, anticipating the day they'll revise it and, better yet, anticipating the day they'll send the text out into the world. When I am creating a version of the writing process for a class, I look for indications that the version of the writing process that I imagine for them matches what they can do with only a little support. I want to see that children are productive, engaged, and purposeful throughout the entire process.

Provisioning a Writing Workshop

ECADES AGO, when I wrote the first edition of the now classic *Art of Teaching Writing* (1994), I emphasized the importance of keeping workshops simple and predictable, and although my thinking on many things has changed over all these years, this injunction continues to be an important one. Back then, I wrote:

> If the writing workshop is always changing, always haphazard, children remain pawns waiting for their teacher's agenda. For this reason and others, I think it is important for each day's workshop to have a clear, simple structure. Children should know what to expect. This allows them to carry on; it frees the teacher from choreographing activities and allows time for listening. How we structure the workshop is less important than that we structure it. (25–26)

> I used to think that in order to teach creative writing I needed to have a creative management system. I thought creative environments, by definition, were ever changing, complex, and stimulating. Every day my classroom was different: one day we wrote for ten minutes, another day, not at all; sometimes students exchanged papers, and other days they turned them in; sometimes they published their writing, sometimes they didn't. My classroom was a whirlwind, a kaleidoscope, and I felt very creative. Rightly so. My days were full of planning, scheming, experimenting, replanning. Meanwhile my children waited on my changing agendas. They could not develop their own rhythms and strategies because they were controlled by mine. They could not plan, because they never knew what tomorrow would hold. They could only wait.
>
> I have finally realized that the most creative environments in our society are not the kaleidoscopic environments in which everything is always changing and complex. They are, instead, the predictable and consistent ones: the scholar's library, the researcher's laboratory, the artist's studio. Each of these environments is deliberately kept predictable and simple because the work at hand and the changing interactions around that work are so unpredictable and complex. (12)

To teach writing, you need to establish an environment and structures that will last throughout every day of your teaching. The essential premise, one that undergirds any writing workshop, is this: the writing workshop needs to be simple and predictable enough that your youngsters can learn to carry on within it independently.

Because the work of writing is complex and varied, because students need to be able to follow their texts toward meaning, and because you need, above all, to be able to coach writers who are engaged in the ongoing work of writing, the writing workshop in most classrooms proceeds in a similar way through a similar schedule, using similar room arrangements and materials. Managing a writing workshop becomes infinitely easier if youngsters are taught in similar ways through succeeding years, thus allowing them to grow accustomed to the systems and structures of workshop teaching. In this chapter, I describe, in depth, a workshop environment that is predictable and structured and that allows for student independence.

THE ENVIRONMENT FOR WRITING INSTRUCTION

Teaching writing does not require elaborate materials or special classroom arrangements. Teachers who teach in widely divergent ways can all offer children direct instruction in good writing. There are, however, a few room arrangements that especially support the teaching of writing, and you may want to consider arranging your classroom around the shared principles described in the following section. You may also want to consider provisioning your classroom with the materials that will make a big difference in your students' energy and willingness to write, outlined later in the chapter.

Room Arrangements

If I was to take you on a tour of any one of the thousands of schools where writing workshops flourish, you'd begin to notice the distinctive room arrangements even before we stepped into particular classrooms. Even while walking along the corridor, peeking into classrooms, you would see that in most of these classrooms there are spaces for students to gather, spaces for them to write, and spaces for writing tools and resources to be stored.

The Meeting Area: A Space for Gathering

In most workshop classrooms, one corner has been filled with a large carpet (nine-by-twelve-feet or similar size), framed on several sides with bookcases, creating a library area that doubles as a meeting space. These carpets (and the communities that are created as the class gathers on them) are important enough that when I recently met with a longtime project principal after she'd been promoted to the position of a New York City superintendent, she greeted me by saying, "Lucy, you'll be glad to know we put carpets into one thousand classrooms already." Usually, one corner of this carpet features a large chair that in some classrooms is referred to as "the author's chair," in honor of the times children sit there to read their work aloud (although in truth the teacher sits in this chair the most). Always, teaching equipment will be nearby the chair, including an easel with chart paper, markers, and a fine-tipped pointer. The important item is not the easel but the pad of chart paper. Most teachers have a couple of charts going at all times, and the teaching point from each day's writing workshop is generally added onto one of the charts. The main chart that threads through a unit of study and is referred to in many of the minilessons in a unit is often called an "anchor chart." Each unit's anchor chart will be prominently displayed in a writing workshop classroom, with other charts around the room. The "anchor chart" from one unit of study is often built on in another unit of study, especially if the two units support the same type of writing. Often there is an envelope near a chart containing small replicas of the chart. Students are encouraged to tape a miniature chart into their notebooks or onto their desks.

It's not only charts that need to be displayed but also published texts and examples of student work and the teacher's demonstration texts. These are, of course, featured on bulletin boards, but it is also important for teachers to have a way to draw attention to particular aspects of texts during whole-class study. The Common Core State Standards' emphasis on close reading and evidenced-based instruction has made it all the more important for students to be able to make specific references to a text while discussing it. To help the class study texts closely, teachers try to have a document camera, an overhead projector, or a Smart Board nearby during minilessons, with a ready wall or screen on which to project enlarged texts. It is very inconvenient to move tables and chairs each time an overhead projector is needed, so you'll see that in most classrooms a permanent lodging spot has been found for the equipment, one that doesn't require a lot of reshuffling to access and use it. For example, an overhead projector is often on a low table alongside the easel, angled toward the wall.

When children gather for minilessons or share sessions, they may sit in a clump or in rows on the carpet but, either way, drawn as closely as possible around the teacher. Most teachers assign children spots on the rug, moving the children who might otherwise sit on the fringes into positions that are front and center. Each child sits beside his or her long-term partner. Many teachers assign one child in each partnership to be Partner 1, the other, Partner 2, and often designate which is to take the lead during brief partner interactions within a minilesson.

Work Areas: A Space for Writing and Conferring

Although the meeting space is important in these classrooms, the most important thing is the rhythm of students sometimes pulling close around the teacher for a short stretch of clear, explicit instruction, followed by them dispersing to their work places, with the teacher now meeting with individuals and small groups as children write. That is, the rhythm in a writing classroom is not three minutes in which the teacher talks, elicits, and assigns; five minutes in which students work; then three more minutes in which the teacher again talks and assigns, followed by five more minutes of "seat work." Instead, teachers teach explicitly for approximately ten minutes, and then students disperse to work on their writing for forty minutes.

It is critical, then, to think about room arrangements that can support students working for long stretches of time and that will allow you to move among the students to confer.

In many classrooms, children work at tables or at desks clustered together to form tablelike seating arrangements. (It is important that teachers check out the relative positions of chairs to writing surfaces to make sure that no student is writing at armpit level. Try this yourself, and you'll see it is extremely difficult to do!) During writing time, students often sit beside their writing partner. Partnerships generally last across a unit of study. Many teachers ask students to sit in "assigned writing spots" during writing workshop. These spots may be different from students' permanent seats, something that is possible because children own only the insides of desks, not the top surfaces, which are shared real estate. When children work at tables, not desks, the classrooms tend to provide each child with a cubby in lieu of a desk. Most classrooms also have a few desks that stand alone and are sometimes referred to as "private offices."

Sometimes teachers tell us they do not have space enough for a carpeted meeting area or for children to work at clusters of desks or at tables. Although

this may sound strange, in more than a few classrooms, teachers create more space by foregoing some of their chairs. They usually do this by unscrewing the bottom half of the legs on a table or two, making those tables low enough for children to sit around without chairs—an arrangement that creates space in an otherwise crowded classroom and also allows children to sit in different ways at different times of the day. The low tables are either near the carpeted meeting area/library corner or in a nook of the classroom, and children who work at these tables kneel or sit on their bottoms, sometimes with rug squares for luxury! In some classrooms, table lamps on these tables create a soft glow.

If you worry that when students are scattered around the room, working at tables or in clusters of desks, they won't all be able to see whatever frontal teaching you do, there are a number of possible solutions. First, you can make a habit of convening students when you want to teach from the front of the room. In classrooms that explicitly teach students to make rapid transitions, it can take no more than three minutes for children to shift from sitting in their work areas to sitting in the meeting area, and of course, you are likely to get far better attention from students if they are pulled closer to you. That option may not work for you, so another choice might be to teach students that when you are about to do some front-of-the-room instruction, the students sitting at tables far from the spot in which you stand know that they are expected to quickly shift their seating spot, coming to a place where they can see you. Others can remain in their seats.

Of course, you can teach writing well while maintaining a whole array of different room arrangements. So although I recommend that you cluster desks in tablelike formations and distribute them around the room, leaving maximum space between the tables, you can certainly make other choices. I do not, however, recommend that you line desks up into two or three long lines, which makes it almost impossible for you to ever come alongside a student, to sit shoulder to shoulder with that student. That position is an important one when teaching writing.

The Writing Center

When considering room arrangements, you'll also want to think about whether you want your classroom to have a writing center—and if so, what the nature of such a place might be. I think it is a terrific idea to house resources in one nook, designating that as a writing center. I can imagine keeping a three-hole punch there, copies of touchstone texts, paper of different shapes and sizes, books on writing well, grammar guides, dictionaries, and the like. But it is unlikely that you'll want such a center to be a place where four or five students sit to write. Teachers who use writing centers as places to write tend to teach language arts by rotating students through various centers. This is often a way for the teacher to assign students various independent activities to keep them busy while the teacher leads a succession of reading groups. Writing, then, becomes a hands-off, laissez-faire activity. In my experience, students don't become more skilled as writers without explicit instruction.

Materials

When a school decides to spotlight the teaching of writing, the good news is that this doesn't require a whole new cycle of budgets. A teacher really doesn't need much to teach writing beyond paper, pens, and storage containers. Other curricular initiatives often involve an enormous outlay of funds for a whole raft of new supplies, but reform in writing can proceed even if children sit on dirt floors and write on slate boards!

The interesting thing about materials for writing is that although writing instruction does not require fancy materials, the flip side of this is also true. Materials can make an exponential difference. There's hardly a writer on earth who doesn't have a fetish of some sort about the kind of pen or notebook or lined paper or font size or software program that allows his or her juices to flow. And I have never known a writer who doesn't use new tools as lures to help break down patterns of writing resistance.

So I do recommend that if you can do so, ask children to contribute toward a kitty that will fund the supplies your children will like (even if they aren't essential) for your workshop. You can then take advantage of bulk prices.

When provisioning the classroom, you will certainly need to think about providing students with writer's notebooks, a way to store finished and ongoing work that happens outside the notebook, writing utensils and revision tools, writing partners, chart paper and markers, display materials, resources, and the special equipment that you may want to use for particular purposes at particular times.

Writer's Notebooks

Many schools order a writer's notebook for each child; in other schools, teachers show children a variety of optional notebooks and then ask them to purchase their own. They are both viable options. What you will not want to do, however, is to leave all decisions about the notebook in the individual child's hands. You won't want some children to have small, five-inch-square notebooks with a lock and key! The dimensions and binding do matter: the notebooks need to have room for a lot of writing, and the bindings can't keep the pages from lying open on the desk or table while the child writes.

You will probably want to steer students away from spiral notebooks, because they have a "required class work" feel. You're going after a more magical feeling. Ideally a writer's notebook gives the impression that it could have been the notebook of choice for one of the authors that a child loves most. Another reason to avoid spiral notebooks, I think, is that some students (and some parents) have come to associate spiral notebooks full of writing with student journals, and there is a world of difference between what most people mean by the term *journal* and what your students are doing. Journals are often containers for writing that has no genre and no audience (other than perhaps the teacher) and that is never revised, edited, or published.

It is also perfectly acceptable for writer's notebooks to be very simple (the marble-covered composition books readily available at stores everywhere work fine for a notebook), especially if the writer personalizes it. Sometimes writers laminate a collage of pictures and words of wisdom onto the covers. Encourage your students to write messages such as "If lost, return to So-and-So" inside the cover of the notebook. Personalizing the cover of a notebook

> *"Ideally a writer's notebook gives the impression that it could have been the notebook of choice for one of the authors that a child loves most."*

and writing notes that will help a student retrieve a lost notebook are ways to support the bonding process that is so essential. This emotional attachment matters more than one might imagine.

If you want to engineer the choice of writing notebooks, you can match notebooks to writers in a way that allows you to make assignments multi-leveled. To do this, steer your struggling writers (and, if you teach third grade, perhaps steer all your writers) toward slightly smaller and thinner notebooks. For a time, you might also suggest that your struggling writers skip lines, while channeling the rest of the children to write on every line. This means that you can ask your students to write a page-and-a-half entry for homework most evenings while still allowing that assignment to be multilevel. For the writers who have smaller notebooks, the assignment is actually entirely different than it is for writers with notebooks that contain more space for writing.

Children date each entry they write in their notebooks and generally proceed from front to back through the notebook. Writing that is done outside the notebook also needs to be dated and saved. That way, you can readily see the amount of writing a student has done in a day or during a week.

In many classrooms, teachers suggest that the final fifth of a notebook be reserved for the child and the teacher to write about goals, assessments, plans, strategies, and the like. Children can tape checklists into this section and write about the goals they set for themselves and the ways they can go about meeting those goals. Teachers can record plans that are made in conferences, and use this as a place to hold children accountable to meeting those plans.

It will be a challenge to teach students to carry their notebooks (or folders) with them between home and school, not leaving their writing materials (and their writing) at home. You can expect that during one of the first days of the year, you will encounter a student who says, "I left my notebook at home." If you comfort the writer with "That's okay. Just write on notebook paper and tape it into your notebook tomorrow," you will soon find that half your class has left their writing at home. So brace yourself. You are going to need to make this a capital offense! Beforehand, practice in front of a mirror so that

you are ready to display to the whole class your dismay with the discovery that someone has left his or her notebook at home. (Sure, you realize half the class has done this, but don't let on, and the culprits will feel as if they have narrowly escaped with their lives!) Say something like, "Class, I need all eyes over here. A crisis has happened." Then wait until the room is quiet enough for everyone to hear a pin drop. "Sari has *left her notebook at home*." Horrors! A crisis! Turn to Sari. Ask, "Is your mother at home, so if we call her she can bring it over? No—she works? She gets a mid-morning break, right? Maybe we could get her to leave work to swing by and get it. . . . "

Now, of course, you do not really mean to phone Sari's parent and suggest that she leave work to bring her daughter's notebook to the classroom. But the point is that if you play this right, you can communicate that it is a very big deal to forget one's notebook. That evening, the whole class can rally to make phone calls reminding Sari to bring the notebook the next day. People can be lined up to ask Sari, the moment she crosses the threshold of the classroom tomorrow, "Do you have your notebook?" And the bigger accomplishment is that the whole class will understand this matters.

Writing-in-Progress Folders and Paper

In addition to a writer's notebook, each child will need a folder for drafts. Sometimes a student's writing is kept in her writer's notebook and sometimes in her folder, depending on the nature of the writing. Either way, it is crucial that the work is dated each day—perhaps with that day's date stamp. This makes it easy for you to look through a student's notebook and folder to re-create what the student did in the writing workshop on Monday, Tuesday, Wednesday, and so on. Principals often sit down with writing folders as part of their supervision and want to see evidence of children's ongoing work.

Writing folders contain drafts and mentor texts related to the current unit of study. They may or may not contain checklists in which children self-assess and goal sheets. Most of the teachers I know suggest using a two-pocket folder for storing these materials. Usually, during the first week or two of the unit, children will do most of their writing in their writer's notebooks, and during the second half of the unit they will do most of their writing on draft paper that they keep in their folders. Usually when they are writing in their notebooks rather than their folders, only the notebooks travel between school and home, with the folders for any one table of writers stored in a box or a tray and brought to the table for the writing workshop.

Youngsters will also need loose sheets of lined paper on which to write their drafts. For some kinds of writing, these loose sheets will be configured in special ways. For example, when your students are working on literary essays, we encourage you to help them create informal booklets consisting of a few sheets of notebook paper, stapled together, on which they collect their insights about the texts they are reading. Almost always, you'll make a big deal about the importance of writing on one side of a page only so that drafts can be scissored apart.

You can decide whether each student supplies her or his own paper or whether the paper is provided in a writing center stocked with writing tools and materials. In grades 3 through 5, most children like to write drafts on white lined composition paper. Yellow paper is harder to read, especially if children are writing in pencil (which I don't really recommend).

In many writing classrooms, teachers find it helpful to color-dot the folders, so children who sit at the blue table have a blue box for their blue-dotted folders. Sometimes the folders are kept in students' possession and sometimes in class containers. If the folders are in class containers, when it is time for the writing workshop to begin, a table monitor will probably bring the box of the appropriate, color-dotted folders to the appropriate color table. Each student is taught to remove whatever he or she has been working on from his or her folder and then, to keep the workplace clear, to return the folder to its box, which is kept nearby for easy access.

When a unit of study ends with a publication party at the end of a month, children empty their writing-in-process folders. They staple or clip a sequence of rough drafts, mentor texts, and perhaps unit-specific checklists and goal sheets together and file them into cumulative folders. Some teachers send a folder of work home after each celebration and publication party, bearing the name of the unit. Others keep all students' work in a cumulative file. Either way, children begin a new unit of study with freshly cleaned-out folders (although assessment materials often span units). And, more important, work is not sent home in dribs and drabs. Children's work needs to accumulate until the author's celebration. And after the author's celebration, some work needs to accumulate as evidence of children's growth over time. No work should be sent home until the first final draft has been published. And final drafts that have been published should be filed.

Writing Utensils and Tools for Publication and Revision

A wonderful thing about teaching writing is that it is easy to provision a writing classroom! Children need something to write on—and something to write with. Other than paper, the most important tools are writing utensils; although any writing utensil is acceptable, I recommend pens. Pencils smudge and break, require sharpening, are harder to read, and invite children to erase. We want to study our children's rough drafts and revisions, so it is preferable for them to cross out rather than erase deleted sections of texts. Then, too, most of *us* prefer to write in pen rather than in pencil, so presumably children feel the same.

Teachers need to decide whether each child will purchase and keep track of her or his own writing utensils or whether these utensils have communal ownership. If children chip in to purchase a whole-class stash of pens or pencils, and if this stash is used to replenish cans kept in toolboxes, one for each writing table, this avoids the "He took my pen!" scraps. If children write with pencils instead of pens, it helps to keep a can of sharpened pencils at each table and to teach writers that if their pencil needs sharpening, they can simply put it in their "to be sharpened" can and take another sharp one. Otherwise, it is not unusual to find the struggling writers spending lots of time at the pencil sharpener.

There are other tools beside pens that matter. Some teachers like to have date stamps on hand to make it more likely that students date their work. They aren't necessary, of course, but having their work dated makes it much easier to hold students accountable for being productive. Students will be assessing themselves and setting goals, and you'll want to teach them to identify what works, to star their goals, to magnify particular parts of their writing. Post-its or Post-it flags or markers or beautifully colored pens can all help to add accents to particular aspects of one's writing folder.

Materials matter because they convey expectations. When you provision your classroom with envelopes and stamps, you encourage writers to send their work out into the world. When you supply staplers and staples, you channel writers to write more and to write chapter books. When you supply writers with scissors and tape, you encourage revision.

In some classrooms (especially the younger ones), writing utensils and tools are stored in toolboxes, with as many toolboxes as there are tables (or other writing work areas). At the start of writing time, a table monitor from each table sets that table's toolbox at the center of the table.

Writing Partners

Partnerships may not fit exactly alongside folders and pens, since they are not the sort of thing one buys from K-Mart or sets up on the last summer days before the children come into our classrooms. But these social groupings are so critical to the success of writing instruction that I can't resist addressing the topic here. My message is this: divide children into partnerships and give them time to work together. It is quite simple, really.

Usually partnerships last across an entire unit of study—sometimes longer. Writing partnerships are not ability based, where one child functions as the "teacher" and the other the "student." These are two people who can work together to help each other. As mentioned earlier, in many classrooms, teachers designate Partner 1 and Partner 2. The advantage of doing this is that in a particular minilesson, chances are good that only one member of each partnership will have time to share, which means that if children are left on their own, the dominant partner will end up talking all the time and, thus, receiving help all the time. When you've named some children as Partner 1 and others as Partner 2, you can alternate who does the talking or the reading aloud during limited periods of time. Partners do not write collaboratively, but they function as audiences for each other's writing in progress and frequently make suggestions to each other. In some classrooms, when work is published and celebrated at the end of the unit, the partner as well as the writer sits in the place of honor, and both writers are applauded for a job well done.

Chart Paper, Marker Pens, and Easel

One of the big goals of your teaching will be to help your students develop a growing repertoire of skills and strategies that they learn to draw on deliberately as they pursue their own important purposes. This means that it is incumbent on you to make your teaching have sticking power. In workshop classrooms, most teachers have found that they can use classroom charts to emphasize that children should continually draw from their growing repertoire of strategies.

Some of the charts in a writing workshop are one-day charts. For example, in a unit of study on writing literary essays, you might quickly jot some of the theories that your fourth-graders are considering developing in their literary essays. That chart is apt to remain up for a day or two. Other charts, however, are *anchor charts*, as I've described previously, and these tend to represent the cumulative teaching points from across a large swath of the unit. If a teacher teaches two information writing units—say, one at the start of the year in which children write about topics of personal interest and then one later in the year in which children write about a topic the class is studying in social studies or science—it would be expected that the anchor chart from the first information writing unit would resurface in the second. Sometimes anchor charts even travel from one grade level to the next, with teachers saying to fifth-graders, for example, "Last year you learned lots of ways to provide evidence to support a claim." After referencing the chart that accompanied that teaching, the teacher might say, "Would you look at the essay you just wrote and see how many of last year's techniques you remembered to use this year?"

Two of my colleagues have written an entire book dedicated to the wise use of classroom charts titled *Smarter Charts* (Martinelli and Mraz 2012). It is more angled to primary classrooms than to upper-grade rooms, but it is useful to anyone wanting to think about the role of charts in a workshop classroom. In that book, you'll learn these and other tips for making charts that support instruction and encourage independence.

- Make charts with students—if not the whole chart, then a part so that children will remember the content.

- Make sure the heading names a big skill or goal so that children know the purpose of the chart.

- Use visuals (photos, icons, exemplars) to allow children to get a lot of information at a glance.

- Keep the charts current and up during the time children need them so they can access them at any point.

- Decide on the language of the chart ahead of time, considering vocabulary and student reading levels.

- Make the charts interactive. For example, have children add their names (on sticky notes) next to strategies tried or have strategies written on sticky notes that can be borrowed as needed.

- Make charts clear and concise by using simple visuals, few colors, and easy-to-read print.

- Reread the charts often.

- Talk about charts often with the whole class, small groups, and partnerships.

- Periodically revise charts or retire them.

Some teachers turn a magnetic white board into a large writing process chart, with a space down one side for each child's name. Children move their name magnets from one column to another to signal their progress from one stage to another. This chart functions as a record of the whole class's progress through the writing process.

Exemplar Texts

Writers need to read widely, deeply, ravenously, and closely. A classroom full of wonderful writers is one in which teachers read aloud several times a day and the students, too, are engaged readers. Although children benefit from rich classroom and school libraries full of a great variety of texts, to learn to write well, they especially need to read texts that resemble those they are trying to write. And they need to not only graze these texts but also study some of them incredibly closely, revisiting them time and again to learn still more and more. The same text can be used to teach leads; semicolons; character development; showing, not telling; lists; pronoun agreement; and a dozen other things. I've often led workshops for teachers in which I show how one single text can be the source for dozens of minilessons. This means, then, that each teacher needs a short stack of dearly loved and closely studied short texts that he or she returns to over and over throughout the year. It is great if children have their own copies of these texts, but if not,

many teachers type up and duplicate exemplar texts (also known as *touchstone texts*) so that each student can carry a copy of the text in her writing folder for reference. (This sometimes requires permission from the book's publisher.) It is important that the touchstone texts that weave through a year are not the same ones year after year.

Word Walls, Dictionaries, and Thesauruses

Every writing teacher will want to find ways to encourage children to spell conventionally. Most teachers find it helpful to teach children the high-frequency words that constitute the majority of what they write. After teaching children to spell a specific high-frequency word, you might post that word on a large alphabetical "word wall," encouraging children to use this as a resource to help them spell that word correctly, even in rough drafts. Add five new words to the word wall each week, deleting a few that no longer require attention. You might also send copies of the word wall home with children once a week so that children can study these words at home and refer to them in the writing they do there. Word wall words are a perfect source for phonics lessons, because they contain chunks that can be applied to countless other words.

In addition to a word wall, a writing workshop benefits from dictionaries and thesauruses. Writers care about words and are willing to work hard to find just the right one. These tools help convey the message that words matter.

SUMMARY

Writers don't need much: paper, a pen, a place to store yesterday's writing, a few wonderful published texts, a responsive reader of writing in process, crystal clear help in writing well, an anticipated audience—and time. Ideally, a writing classroom has a carpet on which to meet and an easel and a pad of chart paper around which to gather, but not much is called for! Because

> "A classroom full of wonderful writers is one in which teachers read aloud several times a day and the students, too, are engaged readers."

writers don't need much, it is entirely possible for a school system to provision writing workshops with all that is needed, and doing so is enormously important. I've watched writing workshops take hold within a year or two in classrooms up and down the corridors of a school, and when I try to discern the conditions that made it likely for teachers and children to embrace the writing workshop, one remarkable feature stands out: *provisions were available*. Throughout the history of the human race, tools have made us smarter. The wheel, the stylus, the computer—these tools of the hand become habits of the mind, re-creating what it means to live and learn together. Teachers and school leaders, too, are wise to pay attention to the important work of provisioning writing workshops.

As described in more detail in the next chapter, managing children so they work with independence and rigor is a very big deal, and decisions you make about room arrangements and materials can play an important part. Even if your entire focus is on explicit teaching, bear in mind that until children can sustain work with some independence, you will not be free to teach. How important it is, then, for you to take seriously the challenge of managing and structuring your writing workshop.

Chapter 6

Management Systems

T O TEACH WRITING, you need to establish the structures and expectations that ensure that all students will work with engagement and tenacity at their own important writing projects. Otherwise, your entire attention will be focused on keeping kids working—and you therefore won't be able to devote yourself to the all important work of assessing, coaching, scaffolding, or teaching. Yet teaching young people to work with independence is no small feat!

You can start by recognizing that you need to give careful thought to how you will institute the systems that make it likely that your students will sustain rigorous work. When you plan your writing instruction, you will want to plan not only the words out of your mouth—the minilessons and the conferences that will convey content about good writing—but also the management structures and systems that make it possible for children to carry on as writers, working productively with independence and rigor. When workshops have simple and predictable structures and systems, teachers are freed from choreography and are able to teach.

THE IMPORTANCE OF STRUCTURES AND SYSTEMS

Why do so many people assume that classroom management is a concern for novice and struggling teachers but not for master teachers? Is there really a good teacher anywhere who doesn't think hard about methods for maximizing students' productivity, for inspiring the highest possible work ethic, and for holding every learner accountable to doing his or her best? I get frustrated when I hear some people say with disdain, "She has trouble with classroom management."

Who doesn't have trouble with classroom management? How could it *not* be tricky to build an environment in which twenty or thirty youngsters each pursues his or her own important project as a writer, working within the confines of a small room, each needing his or her own mix of silence and collaboration, time and deadlines, resources and one another?

Corporate management is considered an executive skill, and high-level executives are often coached in methods for maximizing productivity. Directors, managers, and executives attend seminars on developing systems of accountability, on providing feedback, on organizing time, space, and personnel to maximize productivity. If the people working under your direction were grown-ups instead of children, the job of managing the workers would be regarded as highly demanding leadership work. But all too often in schools, classroom management is treated as a task akin to doing the laundry. That's wrong.

As a classroom teacher, you absolutely need to give careful attention to methods of managing young people so they sustain high levels of purposeful work. You and your colleagues would be wise to assume from the start that classroom management will be a challenge and to give careful thought to instituting systems that channel your students to do their best work.

And the good news is that you needn't invent systems ex nihilo. Thousands of teachers have worked for decades to develop simple and predictable structures and systems that can free you from constant choreography and allow you to teach.

LEARNING ABOUT THE STRUCTURES AND SYSTEMS THAT FREE TEACHERS FROM CHOREOGRAPHY SO THEY ARE ABLE TO TEACH

I recently visited the classroom of a first-year teacher. The writing workshop was about to begin. "Writers," Manuel said, "in a moment, I'd like you to bring your writer's notebook and your pen to the meeting area. Put everything else away and show me you are ready." As he counted ("Five, four, three, two, one"), children hurried to clear off their workspaces of everything but their writing materials. "Table 2," Manuel signaled, "let's gather." Soon Manuel had signaled four other tables as well, and each time he gestured, his children stood, pushed in their chairs, walked swiftly and directly to the meeting area, and sat cross-legged, shoulder to shoulder with their writing partner. Manuel had soon taken his place in the author's chair.

"Writers," he said, touching his eyes to signal that he wanted children's eyes on him. Almost every child turned in his direction. Manuel then began a ten-minute minilesson in which he named a strategy that writers often use, demonstrated that strategy, gave the children a few minutes of guided practice

with the strategy, and invited his writers to add that strategy to their repertoire. Soon the children had dispersed to their writing spots, each hard at work on his or her ongoing writing project. None of them required Manuel to come to their side and provide a personalized jump start.

As I watched all this, I marveled that Manuel, a novice teacher, was teaching in such efficient and effective ways. I remembered with a pang my first years as a teacher. How did he get to be so good? I wondered, but then I knew. Manuel is the teacher he is because although *he* is new to the profession, *his methods* are not new. His methods have gone through hundreds of drafts and have benefited from the legacy of experienced teachers. This is how it should be!

The best way I know to learn classroom management strategies is to visit well-established writing workshops to study the infrastructure that underlies this kind of teaching. Writing workshops are structured in such predictable, consistent ways that the infrastructure of most workshops remains almost the same throughout the year and throughout a student's elementary school experience. This means that when you visit a writing workshop, you peek in on not only today's but also tomorrow's teaching. In this chapter, you and I will visit a few upper-elementary-school writing workshops when they're in full swing, and we'll pay special attention to the nitty-gritty of classroom management. I'll be at your side on this tour, commenting on what we see together. We'll pay special attention to the management of each component of the writing workshop.

- Managing the minilesson: the beginning of each day's writing instruction
- Managing writing time: the heart and soul of the writing workshop
- Managing conferring: making one-to-one conferences and small-group instruction possible
- Managing the share session: workshop closure

MANAGING THE MINILESSON: THE BEGINNING OF EACH DAY'S WRITING INSTRUCTION
Convening the Class for the Minilesson

Most teachers find that it is helpful to circulate around the room five minutes before the writing workshop begins, saying, "Five more minutes until writing," or something similar. This gives students time to finish up whatever they are doing prior to writing time. The workshop itself begins when you use an attention-getting signal to secure writers' attention and then ask them to convene. It is remarkably important for you to develop such a signal and to teach children that it is a meaningful one. The signal can be obvious. Most teachers simply stand in the midst of the hubbub and say, in a voice one notch louder than usual, "Writers." Some instead ask, "Can I have your eyes on me?" or the abbreviated version, "Eyes?"

Experienced workshop teachers are apt to start the year by demonstrating—acting out—their hopes for how students will gather for minilessons. To do this, show children that you expect them to push in their chairs, to make a beeline for their spot on the meeting area rug, to sit (rather than hover), to handle materials however you expect them to be handled, and to begin rereading the charts containing teaching points from previous days.

Some people soon use a countdown as a scaffold to move students expeditiously along. "Let's take the count of five to gather for a writing minilesson. Five: I love that you are getting your notebooks out of your knapsacks and finding your folders." If there are some materials that you want brought to the meeting area, you may want to hold those materials up, creating a Technicolor illustration. (In other classrooms, teachers always expect each child to bring his or her writer's notebook, writing folder, and a pen or pencil to the meeting area.) Then your countdown can continue. "Four: I love that you are setting your work up in your work spaces so you'll be ready to write, and grabbing the materials you need for the minilesson. Three: Great that you are pushing your chairs in and coming quickly. Two: I love that you are sitting on your bottoms, in your spots. One: Nice to see you opening your notebooks so you are ready to take notes."

Of course, before long this behavior becomes automatic, and you need only say, "Blue Table, please join me," and children push in their chairs, come quickly and quietly, sit in their assigned spots, open their writer's notebooks to the first available page, and begin rereading charts from previous minilessons, while at the same time you gesture to other tables as well. This is very efficient!

At the start of the year, after you call one table of writers to the meeting area, you will be apt to name (for the other writers) what children do well: "I love the way the Blue Table pushed in their chairs, don't you? Look how quickly and quietly they're coming to the meeting area!" If you want students' attention but don't need them to gather—like for a mid-workshop teaching point—you will want to use an attention-getting device. Most teachers simply stand in a certain part of the room and say, "Writers," with a commanding voice. After saying that (or whatever you choose as your signal) give the classroom a 360° survey, waiting for absolute silence and for all eyes to be on you before proceeding.

You may question this detailed attention to how children move from one place to another, and there certainly are teachers who prefer a more organic, easygoing approach. But for lots of teachers, especially those in crowded urban classrooms, transitions can be a source of delay and tension, and neither is advisable. A fiction writer once said, "The hardest part of writing fiction is getting characters from here to there," and this can be true for teaching as well.

The important thing is that you use the signal you settle on consistently and teach children to honor it. This requires that after you say, "Writers," you wait as long as necessary until every child has put his pencil or pen down, stopped talking, and looked at you. At the start of the year, you may need to wait as long as three minutes before further addressing the group.

Some teachers are uncomfortable insisting on utter silence, and therefore they speak over still-murmuring children. I'm convinced you do your students no favors when you collude with their tendencies to ignore your words. If your goal is to teach children that words matter, then your words, for a start, must mean something: when you ask for attention, you should expect that children will comprehend and honor your request. The same children who are "Teflon" listeners, regularly letting instructions roll off without getting through, tend also to be "Teflon" readers, regularly moving their eyes but not their minds over the

> *"Classroom teachers who give careful attention to methods of managing young people help them sustain high levels of purposeful work."*

words on a page, then looking up to say, "I read it, honest; I just don't remember what I read." If you regularly repeat yourself several times to be sure children take in what you've said, you are enabling your students to live as if they have comprehension problems. The first step to remedying this is to develop a way to signal for children's attention, and the second step is to resist repeating yourself.

I find it striking that in classrooms in which the transitions are long and mired in tension, teachers often assume this is par for the course. They shrug and say, "What are you going to do?" as if they assume this is how writing workshops proceed in most classrooms. I've come to realize that many aspects of classroom management are shaped more by our teaching—and specifically our expectations—than by our children's developmental levels. When teachers make a point of teaching classroom management, thirty children can come and go quite seamlessly between the meeting area and their workspaces.

Establishing Long-Term Partnerships

When children gather on the carpet, they usually sit in assigned spots beside an assigned, long-term partner. Because your children will probably also have reading partners and those partners need to be able to read the same books (which consequently means they are ability matched), you will probably make a special point of establishing writing partnerships that bring together children who are quite different from each other. Partnerships comprise two writing peers who can help each other; but there is not one "teacher" partner and one "student" partner. Partnerships last at least the length of a unit of study and often longer (although you may have one or two students who are especially trying as partners, and their partnerships may cycle more quickly than others).

When particular partnerships work well, you'll want to try to keep them in place over time. It's a great thing in life to find someone who can help you with your writing. If children are English language learners, the partnerships often contain a more and a less proficient speaker of English. For new arrivals, the partnerships may be language-based—two speakers of Urdu working together, for example.

Management During the Minilesson

The biggest challenge you will encounter when teaching a minilesson is achieving that magical balance wherein your children are wide-awake, active

participants—and yet their involvement does not turn a tight, economical bit of explicit instruction into a free-for-all, with chitchat and commentary and questions and free associations overwhelming lines of thought. Over the years, my colleagues and I have recommended different ways for you to walk this delicate balance, and frankly, you'll need to do some self-assessment to decide on a plan that works for you and your students.

For years, we suggested that the best way to keep minilessons streamlined was for you to essentially convey to kids, "For ten minutes at the start of most writing workshops, I'll pull you together here on the carpet and I'll teach you a strategy that you can use to make your writing better. For most of the minilesson, this is my time to talk and your time to listen. I'll tell you what I want to teach and show you how to do it. Then you will have time to talk to a partner as you try what I've taught."

I still believe that many teachers would be wise to convey that message and to teach minilessons in which children are essentially seen and not heard until midway into the minilesson. I say this not because I think it is the perfect solution, but because I think the perfect solution is hard for mortal men (and women) to achieve. It is a real trick to allow for more active involvement while still modulating—limiting—that involvement.

But in this series, we go for the gold. We send a more nuanced message to youngsters. We say to youngsters, "I'll often channel you to talk—and then before you finish talking, I'll ask you to hold that thought and to listen up while I make a quick point. This means you need to watch my signals. There will be times to talk to the group, times to talk with a partner, times to talk to yourself silently, and times to be quiet."

Thus, the minilessons in this series offer many more ways for students to be actively involved in the frontal teaching than there were in the earlier units of study books. I'll summarize the ways we involve students, equip you with some tips for modulating that involvement, and explain our decision making around this.

- One of the goals of the first portion of a minilesson—the *connection*—is to involve students. More specifically, in the connection we often aim to help students recall the prior teaching that provides a context for today's teaching. We are likely, therefore, to ask a question such as "What have you already learned about . . . ?" and to set children up to talk to their partner about this. Then we pause these conversations, saying, "I heard you saying . . ." and use that as a way to highlight what children already know about a topic. This little activity is varied in a host of ways. We might read off a list of what we have taught, asking students to point to places in their drafts where they did that work—if they did. All of these little interludes for participation can be perceived, by children, as invitations to tell the whole class about whatever is on their mind—which then sidetracks the minilesson. So you'll want to ensure that invitations to talk are kept brief and to that point and that you channel children to talk to each other early in the minilesson, and not for half a dozen of them to take the floor, talking to the whole group in ways that belabor the start of the minilesson.

- During the *teaching* portion of a minilesson, we often teach by the method called *demonstration*. We do something in front of the class so children can notice how we do that activity—differently than they would probably do it—with the hope that they can come to insights from watching us. The challenge is to demonstrate something that the youngsters are also imagining themselves doing, or doing in their own minds, so that as they watch us they notice how we do things differently—better—in ways that inform their practices. To recruit students to be engaged in our demonstration, we are apt to get students started trying to do the same thing that we will soon demonstrate. We start the demonstration with some guided practice. "How would you do this?" we ask, and get children started doing the work in their minds. Then—just when they are beginning to do something—we say, "Watch me for a sec." That is what it means to demonstrate. For our performance to function as a demonstration, the learner needs to be about to do the same thing, and ready to notice how we do things differently. This requires a keen level of engagement by the learner, but again, this requires that we recruit kids to be on the edge of doing something, or performing something, and then, instead, we take the lead, pointing out what we hope they notice in our demonstration before giving them another chance to try it themselves.

- During the *active engagement* portion of a minilesson, students' engagement of course increases. After demonstrating, the teacher then says, "Your turn," or something to that effect, to signify that this is the active engagement section of the minilesson. Teachers set children up to be fully engaged during this time; usually this means either to "write-in-the-air" or "turn and talk" with a partner. For example, if the minilesson centers

on how writers sometimes reread drafts, looking at action words and asking, "Is this the precise word I want to use?," the teacher would probably demonstrate by rereading a few sentences from a draft in front of the class, pausing at each action word, and musing aloud over whether it was the exact, precise word. Then she'd say to the class, "So let's try it." She might set the class up to continue rereading the text, saying, "If you find a place where I used a generic word instead of a precise one, would you write-in-the-air, showing your partner how you'd revise my draft?" thereby channeling children to say aloud the word they recommend substituting. Alternatively, the teacher could ask children to notice and then discuss in pairs the steps she went through to replace a generic term with a precise one: "What steps did you see me taking when I replaced *went* with *crept*? Turn and talk with your partner."

There are some messages you will want to send children about your expectations during the minilesson. Children need to know what to do if a partner is absent (join a nearby partnership, without asking you to problem solve). They need to know that during a minilesson, their job is to listen and look unless you signal for them to do something different—to talk to a partner, to write-in-the-air, to do some fast writing, to list across their fingers. They probably need to know that there will be times when you ask for students to just say their thoughts into the air, into the group, but that generally, if you are talking, you don't expect them to call out. If that is a message you want to convey—and I suggest you probably do—then be careful not only to say that explicitly to your students but also to hold to it. That means that even if your very most amazing student calls out something brilliant during the minilesson, you'll want to signal that, actually, this is not a time for kids to say whatever thought crosses their mind. Of course, there will be times for children to talk in a minilesson—often to their partners—so you will want to show them how to make a fast transition from facing forward and listening to facing their partner and talking. They can't spend five minutes getting themselves off the starting block for a turn-and-talk (or a stop-and-jot), because the entire interval of that interlude usually lasts no more than three minutes!

All of these things are worth explicitly teaching. I've watched teachers practice the transition from listening to talking to a partner by saying, "What did you eat for breakfast this morning? Turn and talk," and then, after a minute, saying, "Back to me." If you take just a minute or two to coach into the behaviors you want and then remember to hold to those expectations later, you'll find this all pays off in giant ways.

MANAGING WRITING TIME: THE HEART AND SOUL OF THE WRITING WORKSHOP

While the minilesson sets the tone for the writing workshop and provides students with another teaching point to add to their repertoire of writing strategies, the main work of the day happens during writing time, when students are bent intently over their work, hands flying down the page, or are alternating between writing something, rereading it, drawing a line, and trying that again, then again. It is during writing time that you are free to support, scaffold, and foster students' growth as writers in whatever ways seem most important for each individual writer. In this section, I'll provide an overview of the structures to consider so that your students are not distracted during writing time, including how to effectively send them off to write, the nature of their work, and how to teach and organize for a collaborative work environment. I'll also talk about ways you can use table compliments and strategy sessions to make your presence felt and ways you can support students' writing stamina.

Sending Students Off to Work: The Transition from Minilesson to Work Time

Just as you explicitly teach children how to gather for a minilesson, you will also teach them how to disperse after the minilesson and get started on their work. Students need to learn how to go from the minilesson to their workspaces and then to open up their folders or notebooks, decide what they are going to do, *and get started doing it*. If you don't teach them otherwise, some children will sit idly by until you make your way to that table and give that child a personalized jump start. It's worthwhile to come right out and teach children how to get themselves started writing. Sometimes you will disperse one cluster of writers at a time. While one cluster goes off to work, you may

say to those still sitting on the carpet, "Let's watch and see if they *zoom* to their writing spots and get started right away!" Sometimes you will speak in a stage whisper. "Oh, look, Toni has her notebook open and is rereading the entry she wrote yesterday. That's so smart! I wonder if the others will do that? Oh, look. Jose is rereading too!" This reminds both the dispersing and the observing youngsters what you hope they will do.

Sometimes you will find it helpful to ask children first to envision what they will do that day. "Picture yourself leaving the meeting area. Where will you go, exactly? What will you do first? Thumbs-up if you can picture yourself leaving and getting started," you might say, signaling to the children who seem ready that they can go back to their writing spots. Sometimes you disperse children by saying, "If you are going to be doing [one kind of work], get going. If you are going to be doing [another kind of work], get going. If you are not certain what to do today and need some help, stay here and I'll work with you." Soon you are leading a small group of children who've identified themselves as needing more direction.

Other times you will say, "Get started doing that right here on the rug," and then you'll watch to see when a student is engaged in the work, tapping that student on the shoulder and gesturing to say, "Go to your work spot and keep writing." Again, this allows you to end with a group on the carpet who need some help.

Transitions are smoother if children always know where they'll sit during writing time. You will probably give your students assigned writing spots. You'll want to avoid, however, making it a habit to not only tell children where to sit but to also tell them what to do. This may surprise you. You may think, Doesn't the teacher tell students what to do during the minilesson? Isn't that really the role of the minilesson?

Those are very important questions, and it is true that in traditional instruction, the teacher would use the whole-class instruction at the start of the lesson as the time to show everyone what he or she is expected to do that day. In traditional instruction, during the whole-class instruction at the start of work time, the teacher would assign the day's work, perhaps demonstrate it, and then youngsters could practice that work in the minilesson, with support, before being sent off to do that same thing with more independence during work time. But during a workshop, your whole-class instruction aims to add to students' repertoire, teaching them how to do strategies that they will then draw on over and over as they write. So you generally end your minilesson by saying, "So when you are ready to work on your ending, remember this tip . . ." or, "So remember that today, one of your options is to do [whatever you've just taught]. But you can also draw on all you've learned to do, prior to now." That is, fairly often students will leave the minilesson and still need to reflect on their progress, consider their goals, review their draft, and choose a way of proceeding. Some students aren't accustomed to making choices about how they will go about tackling a problem, and they'll show this by waiting, as if paralyzed, for you to tell them what to do.

In a classroom in which children tend to wait for individual jump starts, I suggest teachers forcefully get themselves out of the role of making individual work plans for writers. It can help to just say to children, "At the start of each day's writing workshop, I won't be available for conferences. Instead, this is a time for you to make some decisions on your own and for me to admire and record the ways you get yourselves started in your writing."

Leaving youngsters to make their own decisions will be most challenging if they are in the revision phase of writing. You'll want to specifically teach them how to make decisions and plans. For example, I usually tell children that if one is not sure what to do as a writer, the wisest course of action is to reread recent writing and think, What does this piece need me to do next? I also suggest that if they are stymied, they can look at charts for strategies that writers often use and decide which of those strategies might work at that point for their particular piece. Alternatively, they can review their goal, and set to work trying to achieve those goals. In some classrooms, youngsters are expected to give themselves an assignment (also referred to as a planning box) each day. "Decide what you are going to do, record your plans in a self-assignment box, and get started! Walter Dean Myers doesn't wait for a teacher to appear at his elbow and to say, 'You can start now,' and you don't need to do that either."

The Nature of Children's Work during the Writing Workshop

The rule during a writing workshop is that during writing time, everyone writes. So there is no such thing as being "done." If a writer completes one thing, then he or she begins the next thing. On a given day, a writer might progress through a sequence of writing work. For example, a writer might study a few exemplar leads, try a few leads, select one, and start a draft. This means, of course, that the decision making that I described earlier is something that writers engage in throughout the writing time, and it means that throughout the writing time, you'll want to be ready to support your students in being metacognitive, strategic writers.

You should expect that as your young writers progress along through their sequence of work, many of them will come to places where they feel stymied. "I'm stuck," they will say. If you set aside some time to do your own writing, you'll find that you also come to a place where you say, "I'm stuck." This is entirely normal.

When a youngster feels stuck, the first instinct is usually to find the teacher and ask, "What should I do next?" You will want to approach those interactions being clear that your job can't be to dole out all the little steps that every writer is to take. A big part of writing is assessing one's own work, identifying challenges, reviewing possible strategies for responding to those challenges, trying one, assessing how that effort works, and so on. You will not want to remove that entire responsibility from your students' shoulders by allowing them to make you decider-in-chief.

When students come to you with their writing in hand and say, "I'm stuck. What should I do next?" or any variation on that message, you will want to explicitly teach them to be self-reliant. In minilessons, you can teach them what they can do when they feel stuck—or when they are done or when they don't know how to start writing or when they don't know how to revise. Almost always, you'll respond to these requests for assistance by either turning students back onto their own resources or by teaching them to assess and to identify goals, and by teaching them several possible strategies they might draw on to reach those goals. That instruction can occur in a conference or in small-group work. Both are described in more detail in Chapter 8.

For now, however, let me add that it does help if you have a rough plan in mind for how you hope students are progressing through the writing process. If, for example, you are teaching fourth-graders during the personal and persuasive writing unit, you will want to approach your teaching with a pretty clear sense of the approximate path you expect writers to take. If your intention is for writers to take a little more than a week drafting one well-developed essay, you will probably want your students to collect entries for a while—most of Bend I—often collecting more than one entry a day. Then you may expect students to take a day to draft and revise thesis statements and plans for an essay. Then you'll expect writers to work for a day or two to develop body paragraphs. If you enter a unit with a fairly clear sense of the progression that you expect students will experience as they work toward the piece of writing, you can avoid doing things such as teaching students so many good ideas that they never get off the starting block.

Of course, even when a unit is built around some expectations for student work and student progress, things won't go as planned. Every writer is always encouraged to use his or her judgment, making decisions about what the piece of writing needs and letting the piece of writing and the writer's own hopes come together in an individualized work plan.

Teaching and Organizing So That Children Rely on Each Other

If youngsters seem overly reliant on you for direction, you will probably want to teach them to help each other. "Writers, can I stop all of you? Would you look at all the people following me! I feel like a pied piper. Writers, today I want to teach you that there is not just one writing teacher in this classroom. Each one of you can be a writing teacher. And you need to become writing teachers for each other because this is how we learn to become writing teachers for ourselves—in the end, every writer needs to be his or her own writing teacher. So, right now, let me teach you what writing teachers do for each other. Then those of you in this line behind me can help each other."

Of course, it is helpful for you to think about exactly what it is that you think children in your particular class *can* do for each other. At a minimum, writers can listen to each other talk about their subjects, so that may be the first thing you want to coach writers to do for each other. The first step in helping writers do this is to teach them to ask open-ended questions. "Your job is to ask me questions that get me to talk at length about my subject. Ask questions that get me teaching you about the aspects of my subject that are important to me. Let's try it. I'll be a writer. 'I'm stuck. I don't have much to say. I wrote about the Boston Tea Party but nothing much happened, they just threw tea in the ocean.' Remember, your job is to ask me questions to get me talking."

One child asks, "Was it at night?" This is a closed question, and because you want children to ask open-ended questions, you might answer curtly,

"Yes." Your hope is that if you do not reward the question with a rich response, the youngster might glean something about closed questions.

"Were the people who owned the tea mad?" Again, the question doesn't call for an expansive answer, so you might simply bark out a "Yes."

Eventually, a student will ask a more open-ended question: "What are some of the interesting things you know about the Boston Tea Party?" Respond in a dramatically different way. "Oh! I'm glad you asked. I have learned that some of the people who threw tea overboard wore costumes, dressing up as Native Americans. These were the wealthier people in society. Others, the less wealthy, came without special costumes." Children probably will have missed what you just tried to demonstrate, so you'll come right out and name what you've done. "Do you see, writers, that Jeremy asked the kind of question that got me really talking? He didn't ask a yes-or-no question. Instead, he asked, 'What are some of the interesting things you learned?' That's so helpful, because now I have ideas for what to write. And he could help me get even more ideas if he asked follow-up questions. Try it, Jeremy. Ask me to be more specific."

Students not only need to be taught to help each other in peer conferences, but they also need a structure that allows them to do this. In some classrooms, children shift between writing and conferring as needed, and this can be workable. Sometimes, however, if children have standing permission to shift between writing and conferring, very little writing is accomplished, in which case you might wisely insist that writers work silently, conferring only in specified areas of the classroom. For example, some teachers set two pairs of chairs up along the margins of the room; as long as two chairs in the "conference alley" are open, a writer and his or her partner can decide to meet for a five-minute conference (some teachers keep a timer in the conference areas to enforce this time constraint; others add the timer only if the length of conferences becomes a problem).

In addition to student-initiated conversations, you will often ask the whole class to meet with their partners to discuss something specific. Often these partner conversations follow a mid workshop teaching point or come at the end of a writing workshop. Most writing workshops are punctuated midway through by the teacher standing up in the middle of the workshop hubbub, signaling for attention, and then giving a pointer. For example, "Most of you are having your character talk, including dialogue in your story, and that's great. But today I want to remind you that dialogue needs to sound right to the ear. It needs to sound like something a real human being would say. Get with your partner and read your quoted sections aloud to each other. Ask, 'Does this *sound like* a real human being is talking?' If it doesn't, see whether you can alter the quoted section so that it does." A mid-workshop teaching point like this sets partnerships up to talk with each other briefly about a topic the teacher specifies. Similarly, at the end of the writing workshop, teachers often ask partners to share with each other. "Find a place where your character's talk really rings true, and read that aloud to your partner. Then look together at what you've done and try to dissect why it worked." Of course, sometimes these interactions are more open-ended: "Writers, would you tell your partner what you did today to meet the goals you set for yourself?" or "With your partner, will you compare the writing you did today with the on-demand assessment piece you wrote two weeks ago and help each other make sure your writing is getting a lot better?"

Using Table Conferences and Strategy Lessons to Keep the Class Productive as a Whole

During a writing workshop, you will alternate between leading small-group work and conducting brief conferences. The small groups will be especially important on days when everyone seems to need some direction. If, for example, you have just taught children that essayists elaborate on their thesis statements by making two or three parallel claims, each becoming the topic sentence in a support paragraph, you can anticipate that a third (or even half) of the class will need hands-on help translating your instructions into actions. With such a large-scale need for help, you will probably decide to blanket the room with "table conferences." Instead of gathering selected children together, you can go from one table to another, ask for the attention of all the writers at that table, and then confer with one student who needs help while the others watch. Of course, the others will not want to watch unless you shift back and forth between conferring with the one child in a way you suspect will help others as well and debriefing. Do this work in a manner that helps not only the focal child but all the others who need similar help: "Do you see how Anthony just did such-and-so? Try doing the same thing right now." Then, as the children begin emulating Anthony's first step, I can help Anthony proceed to another step, one that the observing children see with only peripheral vision. Soon I'll point out to the table full of listeners that they, too, can do the work Anthony has just done.

I often blanket the room with table conferences during the first few days of the writing workshop and again at the start of each unit of study. At these times, there is a reasonable chance that writers are all at the same place in their work, which is less likely in the midst of a unit of study.

Another way to reach lots of writers efficiently is to sort them into need-based groups and to gather each group for a brief strategy lesson. Again, I describe the methods and content of these lessons elsewhere; for now, the important thing is that you can easily lead four small-group strategy lessons in a single day. These are not formal events. Usually you convene the first group based on the student work examined the night before. Toward the end of the minilesson, I am apt to call out a list of names and say, "Will these writers stay on the carpet after the minilesson?" Then I talk to this group. "I looked over your writing last night and I want to make a suggestion to all of you." I might show this group how they can get past their impasse and ask them to try what I suggested or demonstrated while they continue sitting together. As these children get started, I might move around the room, ascertaining what other children need. If I notice, for example, one child who is writing without any punctuation, I might think to myself, I wonder if there are others like this child? Finding others with similar problems, I might gather this group. "I've been looking over your writing, and I have one thing I want to teach you and to ask you to do." While this second group gets started, I might return to the first group. I might check in with each member of the group quickly, then say, "Can I stop you?" and make a point or two that pertains to them all. Alternatively, I might decide to confer with one child while the others watch, making sure I pause periodically to extrapolate larger points from this one situation.

Sometimes, instead of setting out to lead small-group work, you will intend to conduct one-to-one conferences but then you may discover midway through the workshop that you need to reach more children more efficiently. Therefore, on the spot you shift into leading a small-group strategy lesson or two. You are wise to shift to small-group instruction when you find you are essentially holding the same conference over and over. For example, if I have just helped one child who is writing headings and subheadings for his report to do so in ways that take into account the main ideas he wants to communicate, and then the very next child I approach needs the same kind of help, I am apt to say, "Will you wait for just one second?" while I peer over kids' shoulders to see which other children may need the same help. Signaling, "Come with me," I soon have six children pulled into a tight circle on the carpet. Often I will then proceed to confer with the first child, only now I do this in a way that makes a point to the larger group.

Then, too, if I am trying to confer and can't because I am swamped with children who *all* need attention, I may triage these needy children and work with them in small groups. To one group, I'll say, "I called you together because it seems all of you are having a hard time getting much down on your page. We've been writing for twenty minutes today, and every one of you has less than a quarter of a page. So let me tell you ways that I get myself to write more, and then let's try those ways, because during writing time, writers need to write. One thing I do a lot when I'm having a hard time writing is thus-and-so." To another group, I might say, "I called you together because although you are writing up a storm, and that's great, you are forgetting that writers try to use what they know about conventions as they zoom down the page. I don't want you to go to the opposite extreme and fuss over the shape of every letter and spend twenty minutes looking every word up in a dictionary, but I do want you to become accustomed to pausing for just a second as you write to ask, 'Did I spell that word right?' If you need to, you should be checking the word wall as you write." I can also convene children who spend too long in their peer conferences, who never seem to light upon topics they care about, who forget their writer's notebook, who summarize rather than story-tell in their narratives, who let dialogue swamp their stories, or who need to add transitions to their essays.

Supporting Students' Writing Stamina

What if children can't sustain work the whole time? Generally, writing workshops consist of ten minutes for a minilesson, forty-five minutes for writing and conferring (with a few minutes for a mid-workshop teaching point), and five minutes for a culminating share session. At the start of the year, students who are new to the writing workshop may not be able to sustain writing for forty-five minutes. If some youngsters are not accustomed to

writing for this length of time, after fifteen minutes the class will become restless.

If children have trouble with stamina, part of the problem will probably be that they are doing everything you suggest they do in such an underdeveloped fashion that the work is done within ten minutes. In that case you may decide to give them a series of additional directions (via mid-workshop teaching points) that will sustain them for several more short intervals. A steady rhythm of mid-workshop teaching points that perhaps allows for children to talk with a partner for a few minutes and that also gives them a break from the physical act of writing can tide writers over so they can work for longer than would otherwise be possible.

You may also decide that for a few weeks at the start of the year, your writing workshops will be briefer than they'll be once children have developed more stamina. Just don't let abbreviated work periods become the norm. Children will never write well if they are accustomed to writing briefly. Elaboration is one of the very first and most foundational qualities of good writing.

If you see that even after your children have been in a writing workshop for a month or two, they are still not producing even a page a day during writing time (and more text at home), then you'll want to intervene to increase the volume of writing they do. Start by talking up the fact that writers, like runners, set goals for themselves and then ask children to push themselves to write more. Then during the workshop, go around cheerleading children to write more. Make stars or checks on their pages when they produce a certain amount of text. Watch for when a child is pausing too much, and whisper, "Get going!" Midway through the workshop, intervene to ask children to show with a thumbs up or thumbs down whether they've produced the amount of text you're championing. Use share sessions as a time to count (and even to graph) how many lines of text each writer produced. Solicit children who have increased their volume to talk about what they did to reach this goal. Make charts of "Strategies for Writing More."

Eventually, if some children aren't getting enough writing done during writing time, ask them to return to their writing at another time of the day—during

> *"Your writing conferences can be angled so that you are teaching children how to carry on with independence."*

recess, before or after school. Say, "You wouldn't want days to go by without getting a chance to write at least a page." or "Writers do this. Writers set goals for themselves. Sometimes it does take them a while to get the words on the page, but that's okay. They just rearrange their day so that somehow they get the chance to write." You'll find that the amount of writing your children do can be transformed in short order if you go after this goal with tenacity, and the same is true for almost any goal you take on!

MANAGING CONFERRING: MAKING ONE-TO-ONE CONFERENCES AND SMALL-GROUP INSTRUCTION POSSIBLE

When you confer and lead small groups, you will probably find it works best to move among children, talking with them at their workplaces, dotting the room with your presence. Although you won't come close to reaching every child every day, you can hold individual conferences with three children a day (four or five minutes per conference) and also lead several small groups (they don't require more time than a one-to-one conference), and this will allow you to be a presence in every section of the room. You make your presence matter more because, when talking with one child, you can encourage nearby children to listen in. For most of a conference, you'll probably want to deliberately ignore those listeners, looking intently into the face of the one child, which often spurs the listeners to eavesdrop all the more intently. Often, as your conference ends, you will want to generalize it to the others who've listened in. "Do any of the rest of you want to try that too?" you might ask. "Great! Do it! I can't wait to see." In Chapter 8, I talk about the internal structure or pattern of conferences and small groups and outline strategies that will help with classroom management. Here I describe conference management practices that help lead children to independence.

Making Sure Your Children Are Not Overly Dependent on You

If it seems that your children are not able to sustain work long enough for you to do much conferring, you first of all need to congratulate yourself for identifying and naming this as a problem. You are far closer to a solution once you have looked this in the eye and said, "This is important."

The next step is that you need to think about ways you can scaffold children's independent work. Your writing conferences, themselves, can be angled so that you are teaching children how to carry on with independence another time. For example, you can be sure that some conferences will begin with a writer coming to you and saying, "I'm stuck." In those instances, your first job will be to learn what the writer has already done, has been trying to do, and has considered doing next. Then you will need to help the writer extend his or her work in ways that make that youngster more self-reliant in the future. "So you aren't sure what to do next? What I tend to do is reread my writing, starring the sections that I think really work and checkmarking the sections that don't work so well. Then I decide which to work on first. Often I start with the sections that work well, and I think, How can I make these longer? I ask, 'How can I make more of this good part?' Why don't you try that now? After this, when you aren't sure what to do, this is always something you can try."

Choosing Whom to Confer with or to Include in Small-Group Instruction

Although the context for your conferences and small-group sessions will be created by the entire fabric of your teaching, conferring itself creates its own organizational challenges. For example, you will need to decide how you'll figure out which child to meet with next and which children to pull together for a small-group session. Teachers develop their own idiosyncratic systems here. Some teachers enter a writing workshop with a little list in hand of writers they plan to see. The list may come from studying assessment charts or conferring/small-group records and noticing the children they haven't conferred with for a while, and from thinking about previous conferences that need follow-up. Alternatively, the list may come from thinking about or reading through children's work and deciding on both children who need help and children who could, with help, do exemplary work that might fuel the next minilesson, mid-workshop teaching, or share.

Personally, although I do enter a workshop with a list of the children with whom I hope to confer, I find it is important to be able to improvise based on the signals children give me. So, if youngsters at one table seem unsettled, I'm apt to confer with a child at that table, knowing that my presence can channel the entire group to work rather than socialize. Then, too, if one child is especially persistent about needing help, I generally assume he needs to be a priority—unless he is always at my elbow, in which case I'll respond differently.

I tell children that if they need my help, they should get out of their seats and follow me as I confer. I find this keeps the child who feels stymied from derailing his or her companions as well; in addition, the children learn from eavesdropping on conferences. The line that forms behind me also provides me with a very tangible reminder of how many children feel confused or stuck at any moment, and this keeps me on my toes. If I have six children in tow, I'm not likely to overlook them for long.

Keeping Conference Records

You will definitely want to record your conferences and small-group work, and it is important to develop a system for doing so that fits intimately into the rhythms of your own teaching. The important thing is that this record of your teaching must help you teach better and help your students learn better. This writing needs to be attuned to your teaching, reflecting, and planning. You will probably go through a sequence of systems before settling, temporarily, on one. Five or six systems are especially common among the teachers with whom I work.

Some teachers keep a page on a clipboard that looks like a month at-a-glance calendar but is, instead, the class-at-a-glance. For the period of time this page represents (which tends to be two weeks) the teacher records the compliment and teaching point of any conference she holds. Sometimes the grid has light lines dividing each child's square into several parallel slots, with alternate slots labeled either *c* or *tp*.

Alternatively, some teachers create a record-keeping sheet that culls some main goals from the learning progression for the type of writing they're teaching, and use it to remind themselves of their goals for children's learning as well as to record their observations of children's work and their teaching. Some teachers use learning progressions and unit plans to create a prewritten list of possible compliments or teaching points and carry these prewritten teaching points with them, checking off what a child is doing that merits a compliment, what they will teach, and what they recognize they *could* but won't be teaching.

Some teachers have notebooks divided into sections, one for each child, and record their conferences and small-group instruction with each child that

way. Others do a variation of this, recording the conferences and small-group sessions on large sticky notes and later moving the note to the appropriate section of their notebook. Some teachers do an enlarged version: they post their conference notes on a wall-sized grid, which reminds every child what he or she has agreed to do and serves as a very visible record of which children have and have not received this form of intense instruction.

I like to record conferences in a final section of students' writer's notebooks, the logic being that this way when I return for another conference, I can look at both the conference notes and the work. At the same time, the child has a very tangible record of the agreed-on work and the pointers I have made, and this is alongside the child's own goals for him- or herself.

MANAGING THE SHARE SESSION: WORKSHOP CLOSURE

You will want to draw on a handful of alternate ways that share time generally goes in your classroom and to induct children into those traditions right from the start. Share sessions fairly often involve partnership conversations, in addition to highlighting the work of one student that the rest of the class might use as a model and celebrating the strong writing work students have done that day. The teacher has a teaching point to make in the share, and she makes it while also helping children reflect on how one aspect of their work went.

When it is almost time for the class to stop work for the share session, a child might circle the room, letting children know it is time to finish up. Alternatively, you could intervene to announce, "Three more minutes." In any case, writers will need a bit of time to finish what they are writing. Then you'll decide whether for this share, you want to bring children to the meeting area, or if you'll want to work with them while they are in their writing spots.

Either way, you'll probably begin the share by talking with children for a minute or two. You may plan to share one child's work, either by reading the child's work aloud or by asking the child to do so. Then, typically, there is usually time for children to talk with their partners. Children may alternately hear the story of a child who tried a strategy the teacher recommended in that day's minilesson. "Nicole reread and, lo and behold, she, too, found that she had left something out, and look at what she did! By golly, Nicole used a caret to fix her story!" But if the share is literally a time to share, it will do so in ways that extend what children did as well. "Nicole found, however, that it was important to not only add information but also to subtract information. For example, . . . You, too, might think about whether you could do this as well." You may recap by repeating something you overheard, but, more likely, time will be running short so you'll simply sum up the day's work and make a transition to whatever you'll teach next.

Alternative Structures: Table Shares and Symphony Shares

You'll probably want another format for share sessions, and you can select the one that works the best for you. Some teachers like to use partnership shares when children are sharing work and use table shares when children are talking over their ways of solving a particular writing problem. That is, if your goal in the share is to encourage children to talk about how they are planning ways to end their stories, then you might suggest they have a table conversation about this. Some teachers use those table conversations as a prelude to a community meeting, which probably involves convening in the meeting area.

Alternatively, you may find that in your classroom, the ritual that I describe as a *symphony share* works well. In this ritual, you ask children to search for an instance where they did something well. For example, you may have taught children that when writing opinion pieces, they need to connect their evidence to their reasons. You may ask children to find a place in their text where they work to convince their reader by connecting their evidence and reasons. "When I tip my baton to you, would you read out one instance when you connected your evidence and reasons?" you could say, and then function like the conductor in a symphony, with one child after another reading a contribution.

Teachers I know have devised a few other alternative rituals for share sessions, and you should certainly see this as one more place where you can draw on your own imagination of what's possible.

Chapter 7

Inside the Minilesson

JUST AS THE ART INSTRUCTOR pulls students together to learn a new glaze or a new way to mix paints, or the football coach huddles his team to go over a new play, so too teachers of writing pull children together for minilessons that open each day's writing workshop.

Minilessons are meant as intervals for explicit, brief instruction in skills and strategies that then become part of a writer's ongoing repertoire, to be drawn on as needed. That is, every day in a writing workshop you gather the learners and say, "I've been thinking about the work you are doing, and I want to give you just one tip, one technique that I think will help with challenges some of you are having or may have soon." Then you demonstrate the new technique and help children get a bit of assisted practice trying the technique in miniature ways, all within a ten-minute minilesson. After this, you send learners off to continue their important work, reminding them that they can draw on the strategy they learned that day as well as those they've learned previously. I've often said that the most

> *"The most important words of any workshop come at the end when you say, 'off you go.'"*

important words of any workshop are those that come at the end, when you say, "Off you go." In any workshop, it is important that the kids know how to do just that. They need to know that after the minilesson is over, they can resume the important work they were doing the day before, drawing on all they have learned all year long and especially over the recent weeks.

Usually for a minilesson children sit in the meeting area alongside a long-term partner, clustered as close to you as possible. This is not a time for children to sit in a circle, because conversations among the whole class are minimal. This is the time instead for you to teach as efficiently and explicitly as possible. So most teachers decide to ask their children to sit alongside a partner, at the teacher's feet, facing the teacher.

Although the teachers with whom I teach often worry over the content of their minilessons, the truth is that if you are teaching and learning alongside a classroom full of kids who are engaged in their own writing, you'll soon find that your mind will brim with ideas for minilessons. The biggest challenge is learning not the *content* of minilessons but rather the *methods*.

THE ARCHITECTURE OF A MINILESSON

While the content of minilessons changes from day to day, the architecture of minilessons remains largely the same, and it remains consistent whether you are teaching reading or writing. The architecture of a minilesson (as we have taken to calling the design of a minilesson) is easy to learn and provides support for any minilesson you might ever write.

Minilessons are only ten minutes long, yet within those fleeting minutes there are four component parts:

- Connection
- Teaching
- Active Engagement
- Link

Connection

Minilessons begin with a connection. This is the "listen up" phase of a minilesson. Although this is a whole-class instruction, when taught well, a minilesson has an intimacy, and that feeling is established in the connection. A connection might go like this.

- "Come close. I've been thinking and thinking about what the one, most important tip I can give you might be, and it is this."

- "Writers, can I tell you a secret? I want to let you in on something that I do when I am writing, something I haven't told too many people about."

- "Last night, I couldn't sleep. I kept thinking about your writing and thinking, thinking, thinking about what I could say today that might help. Suddenly, in the middle of the night, an idea came to me. I got out of bed and wrote it on a Post-it. You ready to hear my idea? This is it."

- "Last night, I was telling my family all about the cool stuff you've been doing. I told them . . . Then as we talked about you, my sister said, 'Hey, Lucy, why don't you show them how to. . . .'"

In these and other ways, the connection of a minilesson signals to children that the teaching they're about to receive is important.

The connection has two parts. It begins with an effort to connect today's teaching to the ongoing work that children have been doing and to the children personally. You want children to know that today's teaching is nestled into their ongoing work. This first part of the minilesson, then, often refers to the anchor chart, which lists what the class has been working on. For example, if a minilesson will teach a new way to revise, you might start the minilesson by recalling all the ways that the class already knows to revise. In the second part of the connection, you say, "Today I want to teach you . . ." and then you name the teaching point that crystallizes the most important lesson that the minilesson aims to teach. At the end of the minilesson, the new teaching point often becomes a new bullet on that anchor chart and the children are reminded that they can draw on the day's teaching point or the larger repertoire of related strategies. Children then leave the minilesson with not just a single strategy in hand, but rather with an expanded repertoire.

Let's look at both parts of the connection, starting with the first part, where you try to connect today's teaching to the larger canvas of your teaching (and to the children personally). Over the years, I've developed a few techniques that I tend to rely on.

In the connection, I often try to recruit youngsters to recall the work that they have done prior to this lesson, which provides the context for the lesson.

If I'm going to teach students a new way to write persuasively, I'm apt to start the minilesson by helping children recall what they already know about persuasive writing. I might, for example, say to them, "You've learned so much about persuasive writing. I'm going to reread our anchor chart, and after I read an item, will you give a thumbs-up if this is something that you do in your writing and a thumbs-down if this isn't something you've tried yet." Then I read the list of techniques for writing persuasively that I hope children are already using and let them know that today they'll have another opportunity to use all the techniques they've already learned—and they'll learn a new technique as well.

There are lots of ways to adapt this general idea. For example, I might say to children. "I was thinking today about all the ways you've already learned to write persuasively. Right now, will you list across your fingers three techniques you use often when you want to persuade your audience?" Then after a moment, for silent thought, I might say, "Turn and talk. What techniques for being persuasive have you already learned?" As children share their techniques, I would probably scrawl what I heard them saying into a list, and then pause the conversations to say, "I heard many of you saying these things," and then I would read the list.

There are more creative ways to accomplish essentially the same thing. "Writers, I've been thinking that for my birthday, I want my sister to give me tickets to see *The Lion King*. The first thing that came into my head to say to her was, 'I want them. I *really* want them. I *really, really, really* want them!' But of course, I know I need to be more sophisticated to actually persuade her, and I thought maybe you could give me some suggestions." Then, after harvesting a few suggestions, I could recap by listing the points they'd made about being persuasive. "So I'm hearing you say that effective persuasion. . . ." And in that way I could summarize a few techniques that children already know about persuasive writing.

In the connection, I sometimes share tiny excerpts of student work and vignettes from working with students.

I'm always playing Johnny Appleseed as I teach, finding one student who does something that can nourish other writers' imaginations of what's possible. But I also keep a file of work from previous years and, frankly, from other people's classes. Children are interested in other children even if I need to preface my

story by saying, "I'm going to tell you about something that one of last year's writers did." I save work that is funny, in particular, and also work that represents problems many writers encounter. For example, when I have wanted to teach children that some comparisons are more effective than others, I have told the story of a child who wanted to describe the sound that the waves make at his beloved beach. The child closed his eyes, re-created the sound in his imagination, and then told me what he planned to write, "The waves sound like a toilet being flushed," he said. I used the story to explore connotations, suggesting the comparison didn't work all that well. When I use an example, I recite the exact words that the youngster said to me. Sometimes I do not actually remember the exact words that were used, but minilessons are much better if we tell stories well, and using the words that a person said makes for a much more lively story, so I do my best!

Notice that oftentimes the work I share is not perfect work. In minilessons, I often want to talk to the class about an issue they're tackling, so it helps to tell a little story about a writer who faced similar challenges. If the story is being told as a cautionary tale about what *not* to do, I don't use the names and stories of children in that class, but instead, children from other years or other classes.

> *"A teaching point doesn't simply name what the minilesson will cover—It crystallizes the most important lesson from the day."*

In the connection, I sometimes tell a story that may at first seem to have nothing to do with writing, but in the end, becomes a metaphor for the lesson I need to teach.

I know that it generally works best to tell a story bit by bit, letting it unfold chronologically. I recently told the story to children about a phone call to my mother. I told them, "She had all these problems that she told me about, and I listened and tried to help. Then we were in the middle of talking when all of a sudden she said, 'I'm going,' and then bam! She hung up! I was holding a dead phone. I thought, 'Where's my thank you and good-bye?'"

The children, listening, were entertained because they generally like to hear little true-life vignettes, but they thought the story was unrelated to writing until suddenly, in the teaching point, I made clear the fact that readers, like people talking on the phone, expect a reasonable ending to a story. This, of course, leads right into teaching a variety of ways that people often end their pieces of writing.

The connection ends with a clear teaching point.

The *teaching point* is the last part of the connection. In the teaching point, you'll crystallize what it is you hope to teach in that day's minilesson. I work hard to make teaching points crystal clear and, when possible, memorable and worth remembering. Listen to a few teaching points.

- "Today I want to remind you that when a writer writes essays—personal, literary, argument, or otherwise—the writer often organizes her opinion and reasons into a boxes-and-bullets structure. And writers of any genre, once they have a rough idea of structure, often try to get the whole piece of writing down on the page quickly, roughly, and then go back to revise."

- "Writers, today I want to teach you that when information writers revise, they often consider ways they can add more, or elaborate. Information writers can learn to elaborate by studying mentor texts, taking note of all the different kinds of information that writers use to teach readers about subtopics."

- "Today I want to teach you that writers vary the pace of a story for a reason. Writers elaborate on particular parts of a story to make readers slow down and pay attention to those specific scenes."

- "Today I want to teach you that essayists gather essay entries. One strategy that works is to think of a person who matters to you, and then list specific ideas about that person. Then take one of those ideas and write an entry in which you think about that idea."

- "Today, I want to remind you that writers, especially writers of information texts, take time to think over the structure for their writing. The structure you anticipate using eventually for a piece of writing becomes the structure you want to use earlier on for your research, so that your notes are structured to allow you to write the report you envision writing."

As you study those examples of teaching points and the scores of others in the series, you'll no doubt see that generally, an effective teaching point conveys:

- What writers often try to do—the goal
- Ways writers can go about doing that—the procedure

Very often, the teaching point starts with a phrase or a sentence about a goal that a writer might take on, and then the teaching point conveys the procedure (sometimes naming several steps) the writer might go through to accomplish that goal.

Notice, for example, the fourth teaching point above states, "Today I want to teach you that essayists gather essay entries." That's the goal. It's followed by the way to do this: "One strategy that works is to think of a person who matters to you, and then list specific ideas about that person. Then take one of those ideas and write an entry in which you think about that idea." That's the strategy. I would not feel as if my teaching point earned its keep if it went like this: "Today I am going to teach you to gather essay entries." Such a teaching point wouldn't be worth posting as a bullet on a chart or reiterating several times within the minilesson. That is, a teaching point doesn't simply name the terrain that the minilesson will cover. It actually crystallizes the most important lesson from the day.

Some Cautionary Advice about the Connection in a Minilesson

When working with teachers who are authoring their own minilessons, there are several predictable problems they encounter with the connections in these minilessons. One predictable problem is that some teachers have been taught that it is better to elicit information from children than to say anything to them in a straightforward way. The result is that some teachers begin the minilesson with a barrage of questions. "Class, yesterday we talked about . . . what?" the teacher will ask. "And you were having trouble with . . . what?" she'll ask. You will notice in the connections we described that some of them do recruit bits of active engagement from students, but on the whole, the minilesson is only ten minutes long, and the most valuable place for active engagement is later in the minilesson, once you have shown youngsters how to do something and now give them a chance to try this out, with support. I suggest, therefore, to avoid launching minilessons with questions, and, above all, to avoid asking known-answer questions in which you're looking for a particular answer. Children can't read your mind, so their answers will tend to take you off in different directions, turning a minilesson into a conversational swamp. You have the floor. Try to speak in interesting and clear ways.

The second problem teachers often have is with grasping the huge difference between a minilesson and traditional teaching. These teachers see a teaching point as an assignment. You can hear this in the language they use. They'll say, "Today I want you to do . . ." or "Today you will. . . ." Those are the words of a whole-class assignment—laying out what you want all the students to do that day—rather than the words of a teaching point. A teaching point lets writers know something that they can draw on often, whenever they write.

If a teacher says, "Today I want you to add dialogue to your story" or "Today I want you to add cross-sectional diagrams to your informational texts," those are assignments, not teaching points. Children may all do this activity, but it is unclear that another time, when in the same position, they will know how or when to self-initiate the strategy.

How different it is if you instead say this: "Today I want to teach you that whenever you want to make your story come alive, it helps if you let the characters talk. A writer can do this by bringing the character to life in his mind, imagining the character walking into the situation in the story, then listening closely to what the character seems to say. Then quotation marks allow the writer to put the actual words the character said onto the page." The difference is not just a matter of words. It's a difference of intent. In a minilesson, you must plan to teach writers something that they can do repeatedly, perhaps today, and certainly for the rest of their lives.

Teaching

When planning the teaching, one of the first decisions to make is whether the instruction will rely on a mentor text or not. Often one or two published texts are woven into a unit of study, with students returning to those texts often to study new dimensions of them. Another option is to look to your own writing. Usually a teacher works his or her way through a piece of writing across the unit of study, in sync with the work the class is doing with its writing. The teacher may actually have completed the piece, but for the sake of instruction, she pretends not to have already written it, rewinding back to the start of the process, so that early in the unit, she might demonstrate how

she generates a small list of possible topics and chooses one. Then later, she might show how she gets started writing a first draft, and so on. Sometimes the class also has a text that they've been writing together, and that text, too, might be woven into the minilesson.

While thinking about whether one of those kinds of texts will be brought into the minilesson, you will also want to think about the method of instruction that you will use to teach. As far as I can figure out, there are only four main methods available to us. We can teach people how to do something in the following ways:

- Demonstration
- Guided practice
- Explanation with example
- Inquiry

To help teachers grasp what it means to teach using these four methods, I often ask them to get into pairs, and I then ask one teacher to teach the other how to put on shoes, and to do this bit of instruction using a specific teaching method. (I don't discuss what those methods might be just yet. I simply suggest teachers do this teaching using a specific teaching method.) After two minutes, I stop the group and suggest that now the second teacher in each partnership teach the first how to put on shoes, only this time I ask the teacher to use a different teaching method. We continue this until people have had four opportunities to teach the one lesson—how to put on your shoes—and then I ask teachers to list the methods they used. As mentioned earlier, I have come to believe we have only four options: demonstration, guided practice, explanation with example, and inquiry.

Demonstration

The most common way to teach someone how to put on shoes is to begin by first taking off a shoe and proceeding to narrate the step-by-step process of putting the shoe on. That's the method of *demonstration*. The teacher may have done the work previously (I may already have had both my shoes tied securely to my feet when I started this lesson) but the teacher undoes that work (usually behind the scenes) to be able to redo the work publicly, this time naming the steps taken and tucking in little pointers. ("Sometimes you need to wiggle your foot from right to left a bit to get it actually into the shoe. Don't step down too hard on the heel of your shoes or it might fold in on you.")

Guided Practice

Second, we can teach in a way that walks our students through the process. Our shoes can stay securely on our feet, and our attention can shift to the learner who needs to start, shoeless. "Okay," we say. "Start by pointing your toe." Then we wait for the sock-footed learner to do that action. "That's it. Now stick that pointed toe right into the shoe, all the way to the far end of it." That's *guided practice*.

During guided practice, we guide students so that they have an instructive experience that they wouldn't have had on their own. We engage students in the activity, and as they proceed, we use clear, efficient prompts to coach them along. We hope that once the minilesson is over, they will be able to do the same processes without requiring our guidance or support.

Explanation with Example

We could, instead, give a little lecture, complete with illustrations, to talk through the process of foot insertion into shoe. We could even use Power-Point to make a chart listing the four stages of foot insertion, with pictures to illustrate each stage. That's the method I call *explicitly telling and showing an example*. The challenge when doing that sort of teaching is to make it informative and memorable. Decide on one name you will give for whatever you are teaching and use that one name four or five times in the minilesson. Think of what you are doing as giving students a little speech on a topic. Ask yourself, "What content can I put in my speech?" Will you share a few tips, tell an anecdote that ends up conveying a lesson, use a metaphor to teach a big idea? You'll want to think over how to make your teaching memorable. Perhaps you'll use an anecdote or a metaphor, parallel construction, or a gesture that represents your content. In any case, this method of teaching requires more (not less) planning than the others.

If your explanation includes showing examples, you nee[...] you'll highlight the aspect that is germane. Often you can b[...] into relief by using a case of contrast.

Inquiry

Then again, we can simply ask, "How do you think I got this shoe on my foot? Here's a shoe, here's a foot. Can you figure it out?" That's *inquiry*. This method is most common when you want to engage youngsters in studying an example of good work, or when you want them to contrast effective and ineffective examples, generating descriptors of each. Sometimes this method actually combines the methods of demonstration and guided practice.

Planning a Demonstration: An Example

Each of these methods can be used to teach within a minilesson. To plan how the teaching component will go, I'm going to use the demonstration method as a model, since 80% of our reading and writing minilessons rely on demonstration. Let's say this is my teaching point.

> Today I want to teach you that when you are hoping to convince someone of your opinion, it is important to not only state your opinion but also to include reasons. Usually, the writer states his or her opinion, then uses *because* to include reasons.

To devise a minilesson that uses the demonstration method, it's important to guard against simply telling people about something you have already completed. Such a summary might start like this.

> Readers, I want to tell you that when I was writing my persuasive letter, arguing that the student council should have a role in school issues, I realized I needed to add reasons to support my opinion, so I added the word *because* and then wrote. . . .

That's not teaching by demonstration. That's teaching by leaving your shoe on and simply looking back to explain (and perhaps showing an example). In contrast, if I want to demonstrate, the first thing I need to do is to take off my shoe, or to undo the writing work I have already done, so that I can "put my

...on" (that is, write the passage) in front of the learners. Before proceeding, then, let me share a few other tips about demonstration teaching.

Kids will learn more if you don't try to teach the entire process of writing within one minilesson.

In one minilesson, you do not want to show writers how you choose an issue that matters to you, decide on an audience, figure out what you're arguing for, and also generate reasons to support that opinion. If the day's minilesson is designed to encourage writers to provide reasons to support their opinion, then the only writing work you will want to do is to generate reasons to support an opinion and to add those onto your *already existing* persuasive letter. So to demonstrate only the new part of your thinking, you need to already have a persuasive letter that doesn't include any supportive reasons. So we are getting closer to designing an effective minilesson. The teaching part could start like this.

> Writers, you'll remember that yesterday we started this letter to Mr. Prince, our principal. In our letter, we wrote, "We are writing to let you know that we think the student council should have a say in school issues besides just fundraisers and the decorations for school parties.

Then, of course, you could point out that the letter will be more persuasive if you include some reasons.

Kids will learn more if there is a predictable sequence of moves one makes in most teaching components.

Generally in a minilesson—especially one where the teaching method is demonstration—the teacher starts by setting up the context for the minilesson. Often this means showing writers that you have reached a certain spot in your writing process or have encountered some difficulty. Sometimes just slowing yourself down, taking time to think, to struggle, by saying things like "Hmm . . ." helps. That is, something prompts you to reach out for the strategy you will teach.

> I know we want to convince the leadership of the school that the student council would like to weigh in on issues outside of fundraising and

planning decorations for school events. We're pretty sure we want to add some reasons. Hmm, reasons the school should listen to the student council. Hmm. It's not always easy to come up with reasons, is it? I have a trick that works for me. Let me show you.

Throughout the demonstration, it is helpful if you talk about the task as if the students are doing it with you, even though (because this is teaching by demonstration), in the end, you demonstrate in front of them. You might go further by asking kids to join in the demonstration, like this.

> Try this. Try saying our opinion and then adding the word *because*. Sometimes reasons come to the mind when writers do that. "We want the student council to have more say because . . . A, and also because . . . B." Let's all see if we can come up with some reasons, okay? "We want them to have more say because. . . .

Then you model. You do the work that you want to show youngsters how to do. When doing that work, you will want to sometimes mess up in ways that you know youngsters will also mess up and then correct yourself, giving you more opportunities to teach. For example, you might say:

> "'We want them to have more say because they should have more say.'" No, wait, I have to remember to tell details. Let me try again. "We want the student council to have more say because there are rules many kids think aren't right, like no outdoor recess when it is raining."

Finally, you will want to explicitly name the steps you took in a way that is replicable to another day and another piece.

> Writers, did you see that to come up with reasons, I just named our opinion, "We want the student council to have more say . . ." and I added the word *because*, and just saying that got reasons to come to mind? When we wrote those reasons, we made sure to remember that good writing is detailed.

Kids will learn more if they are trying to do—*wanting* to do—something that you demonstrate.

Brian Cambourne, the great Australian educator, once told me that people fly hang gliders over the field outside his office. On many days, he can look out his office window and see the people strapping themselves into harnesses and running pell-mell toward a cliff, whereupon they launch themselves over the cliff and into the air. Brian pointed out that although he has watched this perhaps several hundred times, those hang gliders aren't functioning as mentors to him because never in a million years would he imagine himself doing what those people are doing. So he watches with detachment, not with intensity as one would in a useful demonstration. In this example, there is a thin line between guiding students to do some work and the teacher demonstrating that work, and that thin line is characteristic of many demonstrations. Often the teacher recruits youngsters to join him in doing something, and then at some point, just when the kids are also engaged in the work, the teacher pulls ahead, performing the work for the students in ways that highlight how he hopes they will all go about doing the work.

Active Engagement

After you teach something, you'll want to give children the opportunity to try what you've taught. Usually you'll do this by involving them in a bit of guided practice in which they do what you've taught while you interject quick prompts that scaffold them through the steps of what you want them to do or that lift the level of what they are doing. Setting this up takes some doing. Here are some options that are available to you, followed by potential problems to anticipate and solve.

Children continue the work on the next part of the demonstration text.

Sometimes, it works out for children to help out with the next bit of work on the demonstration text. For example, in the example described earlier, the teacher has demonstrated how to go about adding one reason to support the opinion, and certainly the most obvious active engagement would be to channel children to turn and talk, helping each other generate other reasons that could be added. As those children talk with each other, the teacher would probably remind them that to be persuasive, writers need their reasons to be detailed.

"Throughout a demonstration, it can be helpful to talk about the task as if the students are doing it with you."

Children transfer what they have learned to do to another class text.

Imagine that the minilesson had instead been about how to title a piece or how to end a piece—or about anything else that one does not do repeatedly in one piece of writing. In that instance, at the end of the demonstration, the work on that text would be complete! There are generally a few options. First, often there is a class piece of writing as well as the teacher's own writing that could provide an opportunity for youngsters to try their hand at work the teacher has just demonstrated.

Children transfer what they have learned to their own writing.

Another option is for the teacher to channel children to try this work on their own writing or on one piece of writing from within their partnership. For example, the teacher could say, "Would you take a minute and reread your opinion writing from yesterday, and will you mark the place where you think you need to add specific reasons?" Then, after a moment of work, the teacher might call out, "Partner 1, tell Partner 2 what you might add. Help each other." Alternatively, the two members of a partnership could all along have looked at just one member's work. Then again, the teacher could have shared a piece of problematic writing with the class and recruited them all to pitch in, suggesting ways to improve that piece of writing. If the teacher is sharing problematic writing, she'll often create the text for the occasion and pretend it was written by some mystery student or a niece or nephew. "I'm wondering if you guys could help my nephew to do some of that same work. This is what he has written so far. Would you turn and talk? What tips do you have for what he might do next?"

Children act as researchers, naming what you have done in the demonstration.

Sometimes in the active engagement section of a minilesson, it is challenging to figure out a way for youngsters to practice what you've just taught quickly, and so you might devise an alternative way for the children to be actively involved. Typically, you'll devise a way for children to watch someone else (usually you) doing the work, and you'll ask them to function as researchers, articulating what they observed. You might say, "Tell your partner what you saw me doing that you could do too."

Children find and mark a place in their own writing where they could do the work of the demonstration.

Sometimes, when the teaching component of a minilesson has taught children something that writers do, you'll want to ask children to plan for how they'll do that in their own writing rather than actually doing that work within the minilesson. You might, for example, ask them to reread their writing and find a place where they could do that work. "Mark the place where you plan to do that with a planning sticky note that reminds you of your plans."

Predictable Problems during the Active Engagement

There are a few predictable problems you may encounter during the active engagement phase of a minilesson. First, children can spend all their time on the logistics and never do the work. Teachers need to expect problems like these and teach students how to work well with partners and move quickly through transitions. "Watch my partner and me," you'll say, roping in a student teacher so that you can reenact some of the inefficiency you have seen. "Does this look like we're making smart use of our partner time?" Children will laugh, knowingly. Then, for contrast, you can say, "*Now* watch my partner and me," and this time look your partner in the eyes, nod responsively as he or she talks, move quickly to the next item to try, and so forth.

During this stage of a minilesson, the other great risk is that the *mini*lesson will become a *maxi*lesson, and that children won't, therefore, have thirty or forty minutes after the minilesson to actually write. Short active engagements are hard to plan, but we must keep them short so students have time to write! If you wait until each child has completed the work you channeled them to do, or if you respond to all the confusions and questions that children have at that point, or if each child reports back to the whole group on what he or she has done, or if you also need to record each child's contributions on chart paper, this truly creates problems—there is no time left for the most important part of the workshop!

Link

Pulitzer prize–winning writer Donald Murray once told me that the single most important sentence in a paragraph is the last one. "This sentence needs to propel readers onward to the next paragraph," he said. "It needs to be not a closing, but a launch." I remember this advice when I reach the final part in my minilessons. These last few sentences need to encapsulate the content of the minilesson in such a way that kids can carry that content with them as they head off from whole-class, teacher-led work into the whole of their writing lives.

The challenge always when teaching is to make a real difference—a challenge that is not for the faint of heart. It's a tall order indeed to believe that we can call students together, take five or ten minutes to teach a technique, and expect they'll actually add that technique to their repertoire, using it later and even again much later when the time is right. It is crucial to remind children that the particular teaching point of that day is part of a larger repertoire of strategies that they will be drawing on. This often means that in the link, you will refer to an anchor chart (presumably the same one that was mentioned in the connection). When doing this, you'll want to remind children that the goal is not just to do the work of the day's minilesson but to draw on what is now an even larger repertoire of strategies. You'll also want to remind them that always, throughout their lives, writers call on a growing repertoire of strategies.

So you'll speak with great energy. "And so I'm hoping that today and every day," you'll say with great solemnity, knowing this repeating phrase may matter more than anything else in your teaching. "Whenever you are in this writing situation, you'll remember you can try. . . ."

The link, of course, also needs to channel students to actually accomplish something concrete today, so this might also be a time for brass tacks: what kind of paper, where is that paper accessible, what one might do first and next, and what is expected by when.

Then there is the actual send-off. It might be that you channel those who will be doing one kind of work to get going, then after letting those children settle themselves down, you might channel those doing a second kind of work to get going. Then again, you might ask every writer to complete something on the rug, and when they have finished, to go back to their work spots.

THE ROLES WRITERS PLAY DURING A MINILESSON

I find it's helpful to teach children what *their* jobs will be in a minilesson. Explicitly. On more than one occasion, you'll say, "Today and every day in the minilesson, when I say, 'Writers, let's gather,' you'll get your writing folder and quickly move to here. Then I'll talk to you for a few minutes. When I talk to you, you're going to *listen*, because I'm going to show you strategies you'll want to use in your writing. You'll do a lot of listening during that first part of the minilesson, and not a lot of talking." This introduces children to the connection and the teaching part of a minilesson.

You also want children to understand the third component, active engagement, and so you'll also say, "Then after I show you something I hope will be helpful to you, you'll have time to try the strategy yourself, right here on the rug. Usually you'll turn to your partner and do some work together. Sometimes you'll be helping to think about a text the whole class is writing together. Then after the minilesson you'll go off to your writing spots, and you'll carry the strategies with you and use them as you write your own pieces on topics you choose." Your little speech doesn't mean children now deeply understand what is expected of them during minilessons, but it will help.

You may find yourself worrying over how you'll generate *the content* for your minilessons, and this will be the focus for much of this series. I'm convinced, however, that it's even more important for you to learn *the methods* of leading efficient, effective minilessons. When you study the craft of effective minilessons, this work can change your teaching not only in the writing workshop but also in every discipline, and it can improve not only your whole-class but also your small-group instruction.

Chapter 8

Differentiated Feedback
Conferring with Individuals and Small Groups

RESEARCH BY JOHN HATTIE (*Visible Learning*, 2008) and others shows that one of the methods of teaching that accelerates a learner's progress more than almost anything is the provision of feedback. If learners receive feedback that contains both acknowledgement of what that learner has begun to do that really works and suggestions for next steps toward an ambitious but accessible goal, then learners progress in dramatic ways. In writing instruction, one-to-one conferences and small-group instruction provide crucial opportunities for you to offer strong, individualized feedback and instruction.

Of course, providing feedback and instruction to students requires that you have time to read student work and to talk individually or in small groups to learners. So the first challenge is not necessarily figuring out what to say in a conference or a small group; it is figuring out how to scaffold and build student independence so that responsive teaching is even possible.

HOW IS ONE-TO-ONE CONFERRING AMIDST A CLASS EVEN POSSIBLE? HOW ARE SMALL GROUPS POSSIBLE?

Whenever I gather teachers together to talk to them about the power of one-to-one conferences and small-group instruction, I find that many have trouble listening to a detailed description of what happens within a conference or a small group because their minds are stuck on the questions, "How is any of that possible? How can you give attention to only one child, or only one group of four? What are the other children doing?" And if I explain that the others are carrying on, writing with lots of independence, it is not unusual for a teacher to explain to me that the population of her school is not accustomed to, and perhaps not ready for, the sort of self-discipline and concentration that allows youngsters to sustain work without a teacher's whole-class attention.

These questions are absolutely critical to the entire enterprise of teaching writing. In fact, I can hardly imagine more important questions. The answers are complicated, and

I will try to be as helpful and as clear as I can be. But I also want to suggest that you will benefit more from the upcoming section if you try to let yourself play the believing game. I think it will help if you temporarily set aside the part of you that says, "No way. Not possible." Try reading the upcoming section with an open mind, realizing that in literally thousands and thousands of classrooms, kindergarten through eighth grade, writers can actually carry on as writers with enough independence that teachers can conduct attentive, effective one-to-one conferences and small-group coaching sessions. And those classrooms *are* like yours. The writing workshop is thriving in large cities, in elite private schools, in rural hamlets, in international schools throughout the world, in public schools in Israel and Jordan, Mexico, and Sweden—including, in some of those countries, schools that have fifty children in a classroom. The key question is *how* is this done, because there is nothing special in those schools or in those teachers' DNA.

Set children up to do work they can envision doing, want to do, and believe they can do.

Your students will be most apt to work with enough independence that you are free to teach if they are doing work (or trying to do work) that they can envision doing, want to do, and believe they can do. If your children all seem utterly dependent on you, perhaps you have set the bar too high, for now. If you want to figure out ways to manage the class so that you are freed to teach, you need to provide students with highly motivating, not-too-scary work for them to do. Engaging students in a sequence of steadily more challenging work is a critical part of any good curriculum, so those of you who rely on these units of study should be in good stead. But it is also important for you to always keep in mind that when students appear especially needy, it may be that you've just asked them to take a giant step forward, and they may be signaling to you that they need an interim step.

Provide clear expectations for the work that students can tackle with independence.

Then, too, make sure you are clear about what you expect students to do for themselves, and don't give mixed signals. Sometimes a teacher will say to me, "I don't know what to do. My kids keep asking for help with _____." My response is always, "That's because you keep giving them that help." If

you consistently say to any child who asks for help, "Your job is to do that as best you can," then children won't find it rewarding to ask you for that kind of help—and they'll stop asking.

If children come to you to ask for anything that is essential to their continued progress, you will want to think about whether you have supported them enough in helping themselves. Is your classroom organized so that only you distribute paper? Provide access to the bathroom? The pencil sharpener? To a partner who'll listen to a draft? Grant permission to finish one text and start another? If you answer yes to any of those questions, you will need to rethink your systems so that students can carry on independently.

This may make you uneasy. How will you know if the draft has been done well enough that it can be pronounced done? How will you check on the amount of time children spend in a conference if you're not in that loop? The answer, of course, is to actively teach children your expectations, to use the free time you gain to check in on how youngsters have handled the responsibilities you've given them, and to teach in response to what you see. That way, you are still able to talk to children about work that has been declared finished and actually didn't match your expectations or about undue time at the pencil sharpener or in the bathroom. But your interactions will be designed to lift the level of this work not just this one time, but in the future.

Actively teach children how to be problem solvers and how to self-manage.

When children come to you hoping for solutions to problems they could have resolved on their own, try to remember that although it may be easy to simply solve the problem, it is wiser to take the time to put yourself out of this job. Ask, "What do you think?" Then add, "So why don't you do that? And next time, I think you could solve a problem like this on your own." Alternatively, you might say, "I'm wondering if you need to come to me. I bet you can figure that out on your own." Your job in the conference will be to help the writer become self-reliant in the future.

This same work can be done in a small group. "I called you guys together because all of you are asking for similar help, so I wanted to talk to you as a group. You're all asking, 'Can I be done?' and I wanted to let you know the sorts of things you can do to answer that question for yourself. The first thing. . . ."

As you do this teaching, whether in conferences or in small groups, remember that you help students become more self-reliant by reminding them to draw on the classroom charts that contain all the tips they've been taught all year long.

THE ARCHITECTURE OF A CONFERENCE

Most of us do not realize that there are times when our interactions with others follow a predictable structure, but this is nevertheless the case. In traditional classrooms, for example, the teacher will often ask a question, elicit a response from a student, and then evaluate that response. That is, the teacher asks, "What is the capital of New York?" The child responds, "Albany." The teacher assesses, saying, "Very good." This pattern of interaction doesn't often occur outside of classrooms and is not generally regarded as ideal. Usually, if a person asks, "What is the capital of New York State?" and learns that it is Albany, the response would be, "Thanks," not "Very good." Teachers who follow this question-response-evaluation pattern of interaction may not realize they are doing so. These teachers may think they are utterly changing their teaching when, for example, they work with new content (asking questions about Vermont, not New York, or about the transportation, not the government of the state) or when they ask questions that require paragraphs rather than simply a few short words of information. But the truth of the matter is that as long as the pattern of interaction in these teachers' teaching remains the same, the instruction itself will convey many of the same messages.

When a teacher confers with a writer, her interactions tend to follow a consistent pattern, one that teachers of writing have deliberately chosen and that reflects many beliefs about learning, teaching, and writing development. So, although conferences *appear* to be warm, informal conversations, they are in fact highly principled teaching interactions, carefully designed to move writers along learning pathways. Here, I hope to elucidate the principles that guide me, and others, as we confer with young writers. Specifically, I'll discuss the architecture of writing conferences. Although writing conferences are intimate, infinitely varied conversations between a learner and a coach, there is a way the structure of one writing conference is very similar to another. Afterward, I'll describe how the architecture of small-group work is very similar to that of a conference.

For any writing conference to work, the writer must first be engaged in writing work. That is, you must first organize and teach the whole class in such a way that each child is engaged in his or her own purposeful work as a writer. Then you observe and coach in ways that either help the learner do what he or she is trying to do or that direct the learner to take on new (and perhaps more challenging) intentions. Either way, once you channel a writer to more challenging work, you usually need to briefly scaffold that new level of work. Then you pull back, encouraging the youngster to continue without relying on you as much.

This means that a writing conference almost always involves these four phases:

- **Research** what the child is intending to do and has done.
- **Decide** what to teach and how to teach it.
- **Teach** using one of four methods, each of which usually ends in guided practice.
- **Link** by extrapolating from today's work whatever it is that the writer will want to carry forward into tomorrow's work.

The predictability of these interactions makes them more powerful because writers can, in the end, use this same progression to confer with each other and with themselves. These units of study books are dotted with examples of conferences. As you read them you will see these principles in action.

The Research Phase

When I try to help teachers learn to confer well, I focus on the importance of research, since that is the cornerstone of effective conferring. If you don't spend enough time trying to understand what the writer is doing and why, then what you decide to teach the student is often generic, perhaps just a recap of a minilesson. That is, when a conference doesn't begin with a teacher taking into account what the child has done and is trying to do, then during the teaching phase of the conference, the teacher often just reiterates teaching that has already happened, unaffected by this particular student and his or her work. Your conferences can be among the greatest sources of originality and power in your teaching, but this can only happen if you are truly responsive. The vitality, originality, and specificity that characterize powerful conferences require that you, as a teacher, take in what the writer is understanding, doing, planning, and working to achieve.

To understand conferring, it helps to think about times when someone has conferred with you. That person might begin the interaction by saying, "Fill me in on what's been going on" or by asking, "How's it been going?" My hunch is there are times when a question like "How's it been going for you?" has led you to reflect on yourself, and your work, in ways that have created dawning insights about yourself and the work you have done so far, and there are other times when the same question has led you to stammer out a robotic or perfunctory answer: "Not that much has been happening, really." The difference in your response to the one question and the other probably has less to do with the words out of that person's mouth than with your sense of whether the person was really interested and sympathetic. When a person really listens, leaning in to hear more, nodding in ways that convey, "Say more," that intense and generous listening leads us to say more. We amplify, we illustrate, we elaborate, we connect. A good conference begins with deep listening.

question the goals. ("I can see you have been working on X, but I want to urge you to work also [or instead] on Y.") When you think about what you'd want from someone who is observing and coaching your teaching, you quickly arrive at a list of dos and don'ts that pertain also to conferences and small-group work with young writers.

Because it is crucial to begin a conference by understanding what the writer has already been doing, you'll usually begin by watching—even just as you approach a writer, or as you scan a table, determining the youngsters with whom you want to talk. Make a point of noticing the writer's all-important engagement in his writing. Glance at the page, at the writer's work spot, trying to glean anything at all that can help you begin to understand the child's process as a writer. The research phase, then, begins with a teacher observing, interviewing, and sometimes reading the student's work to understand what the student is intending to do as a writer.

Observe and interview to understand what the student is trying to do as a writer.

When you want to coach writers of any age, you need to first learn what the writer is already trying to do. You will grasp how important this initial phase is if you realize that the conferences and small groups you hold with children about their writing are not unlike the interactions principals and staff developers have with you about your teaching. It's helpful if the person who coaches *you* first listens and observes to learn what you are already trying to do. Imagine, for example, that you had already spent months focusing on the strugglers in your classroom, and you decided now to nudge your strongest students to do better work. What if an administrator sat in on a few moments of your teaching and blithely told you that you mustn't focus on your strong students at the expense of your strugglers!

Of course, the administrator wouldn't have made that suggestion to you had she prefaced the visit by asking, "What have you been working on?" and "How's it been going?" and even "So can I watch that?" When supervision begins with listening, with learning about your goals, then the coach can either help you reach goals you have set for yourself or the coach can call to

"When you coach writers of any age, you need to first learn what the writer is already trying to do."

Help the child articulate and explain her intentions.

"What are you working on as a writer?" you'll ask. You'll teach children that when they respond to this question, you want to learn not just the writer's content ("my dog") or genre and content ("a poem about my dog") but also the writer's goals and strategies. ("I'm writing a poem about my dog *and I'm trying to be sure readers can visualize my dog, so I'm adding more descriptive words.*")

If you ask, "What are you working on as a writer?" or any substitute for that question, and the child launches into the detailed recap of what she is writing about, you need to stop the child. It is okay to hold up your hand like the crossing guard at your school does to stop oncoming traffic. "Wait, wait," you'll need to say. Then you need to not just steer the child in a different direction but to explicitly say why you are doing this. "When I ask, 'What have you been working on as a writer?' I'm not really wanting to hear what you are writing about, though there will be times when I will ask you to tell me your content. I'm wanting to know what new stuff you are trying to do to get to be an even stronger writer. Like, for example, have you been . . . ?" And then I might fill in some of the answers I anticipate the child producing. "Have you been trying to find a metaphor that captures what you want to say? Have you been rereading to see what images will be especially strong so far?"

You may need to go over what it is that you see the student doing, thereby giving the child words she can use to articulate her intentions. For example, if the child is revising an essay, you might say, "I'm noticing that you are revising. It looks like you are trying to make sure that the examples you use are angled so they make the point you want to make. Am I right?"

Usually once a child has told you what she is trying to do, you'll probe to understand what the child means. If the child says, "Yes, I'm unpacking my evidence," you might say, "Can you show me where you did that?" Or "If you were going to unpack this example, how might you do that?" Of course, you usually have your own understanding of the terms children use (because they use the very terms you've taught them), but it is crucial to help a student articulate what she means by those terms. As you begin to devise a theory about the work that the youngster is doing, it is helpful to follow up on that theory. You might, for example, say to the youngster, "I'm beginning to get in mind what you usually do during this part of your writing process. Will you listen up and see if you agree with my description?"

Of course, conferences occur in the context of previous conferences or small groups, so you can also begin a conference by recalling the last time you and the writer discussed his work, and you can ask, "How has it been, trying to . . . ?" You can then look at progress that resulted from that conversation. For example, you might say, "Last time we talked, you agreed to take the giant step forward of trying to write a whole lot more in one sitting. How has that been going for you?" Then you'll follow up by saying, "Can we look at your work before we talked and since, and compare it?"

Make sure to pursue more than one line of questioning.

One of the rules of thumb that I especially emphasize is this: once you ask the writer a question about his writing and follow that line of questioning, you'll come to a place where you grasp one thing about the writer and his work. At this juncture, it is very tempting to launch into some teaching about that one point. Don't do it! Instead, suspend closure. Don't settle for a single line of inquiry. Be sure to return to a second question, following that one through so that you also understand another aspect of the writer

and the work. If you first ask what the child is working on and learned about her work with the ending of a piece, for example, you might then say, "So one thing you are doing is working on an ending, and to do that you are . . . What are some of the *other* things you plan to do with this piece of writing today?" Of course, that second question could have been entirely different. You could have asked, "How do you feel about this piece? Is it one of your best? Is it just so-so?" You could have asked, "If you were going to fix this piece of writing up so that it is much, much better, what would you do?" As children think about their answers, you'll usually get a chance to sneak a quick look at the piece of writing so that as you interview the writer, you are also drawing on another source of information. One way or another, you will want several sources of information to draw on as you move to the next phases of a conference.

In the research component of a conference, then, you observe, interview, and read the child's writing (though if it is long, perhaps only a portion of it) to understand what the child is trying to do as a writer. Because your goal is to bring your students as far along the writing path as possible, and because you know that each conference is a precious opportunity to teach your students only one of the myriad teaching points available, it is sometimes easy to get stuck doing research fixated on the many things the child does not yet know how to do. Of course you do want to study what the child is not doing to help you decide what new thing to teach, but your conferences will be more successful and meaningful if you take in what the child is working on with your eyes open, particularly to his successes as well.

The Decision Phase

To an outside observer, a conference may seem fairly relaxed. But for me, as a teacher, conferences are anything but. As the writer talks and as my eyes quickly take in the draft and any other available data, my mind is always in high gear. Malcolm Gladwell, the author of the best-selling book *Blink: The Power of Thinking without Thinking*, suggests that he can observe a married couple for just half an hour and predict the chances that their marriage will be intact a decade hence. In a conference, I'm trying to do an equally astonishing feat of "thin-slicing." I take in all the data I can quickly assimilate, and as I do this, I'm theorizing, predicting, connecting this writer to other writers I've known, determining priorities, imagining alternative ways to respond, and lesson planning! All this must happen while I smile genially and allow myself to be captivated enough by what the child says to keep the data coming my way! This is no easy task, and teachers are wise to recognize that this invisible aspect of teaching writing is the most challenging one of all.

In the decision phase of a conference, you'll quickly synthesize what you have learned and you'll think about the learning pathways that the child is traveling along. For example, a youngster is somewhere in a learning progression that relates to the type of text she is making. Relative to that, she is somewhere on the journey of learning to structure that kind of text, to elaborate on that kind of text. You need to ascertain where the writer is on that pathway so you can help her progress to the next step. You might say to the writer, "Hmm. You've told me a lot about your process and your writing plans. I need to think for a moment about what the most important coaching I can give you might be." It is important to deliberately delay acting on what you have learned until you have made a conscious decision. What is it you can teach that will make the biggest impact on this child's writing—not only in this instance but in her whole life? There is no one right answer to this question, of course. In making this decision, you'll draw on the following considerations.

You want to teach every student to become someone who has intentions for his writing, assesses, sets a course, and acts deliberately.

Given that there is no one right way to improve any piece of writing, you'll want to listen to the writer's self-assessment, the writer's goals and plans, and to either teach within the context of the overall direction the writer has set or to talk to the writer about that overall direction. If the child thinks this is the best piece she has ever written and is working to copy it over exactly, you need to know the child's view before proceeding. When it makes sense to do so, you'll want to help the writer accomplish what he or she is already working to do—and perhaps to ramp up or extend those intentions.

If you don't want to get behind the child's existing intentions (or if you can't discern what these are), try to rally the child to take on a new intention and then equip the child to realize that intention.

If a child is writing in generalizations without any detail at all, you could simply elicit details and get the child to record them. But I suggest that instead you try *not* to do that, but rather first teach the child that writers try to write with details, rallying the writer to embrace that goal. *Then* you can proceed to elicit those details and get them recorded on the page.

Responsive teaching doesn't mean that you simply buy into whatever a writer wants to do. Your teaching will be goal-driven. Your goals will come from your knowledge of the standards toward which you are teaching. It is your job to move youngsters to (and beyond) grade-level expectations. Your goals will come also from your own values and resolutions because your teaching can make a dramatic difference in supporting these. If it is important to you to support students' initiative, zeal, and willingness to take risks and to work hard, then these goals need to influence your ways of working in a conference.

Always teach toward growth—and eventual independence.

You will be thinking, "What is the most important way I can help this child to become a dramatically better writer?" You are not asking, "What would I do to improve this draft if the piece was mine?" You won't want your conference to be a time to spoon out a little thing that the child can accomplish within five minutes. Instead you will aim to help the child make a big step forward. On the other hand, the goal is for the child to be able to approximate this important work with independence, so you will balance wanting to challenge the writer with acknowledging that you need to teach what is next on this writer's horizon.

During the decision phase of a conference, you will also decide on *how* you will teach. You'll teach using one (and sometimes more than one) of the four methods described in Chapter 7: demonstration, guided practice, explanation with example, and inquiry.

The Teaching Phase

After you've made a decision about what and how you'll teach, you'll begin teaching. As you begin, you'll want to make sure to name an area of strength, something that the child has done (or has almost done) that has significance in the child's learning journey. You'll want to start by naming this in a way that makes it likely that the child will do this same wise work again in future pieces of writing.

Name an area of writing strength; compliment the writer on a transferable skill or strategy.

To do this, you need to be able to extrapolate something transferable out of the details of the child's work. "I am noticing," you might say, "that you are rereading what you wrote before adding more words. That is so smart of you. Writers do that all the time!" Or "I love how you put so much detail into that image of you and your cousin at the top of the Ferris wheel. I can even imagine your hair blowing in the wind! Writers do that, you know, add as much detail as they can into their writing so their readers can know even more about their stories." The challenge is to notice a very specific way the child has succeeded and then to phrase the compliment in such a way that the child understands he or she can carry this skill into his or her writing work on other pieces and other days.

If the child added into her draft the sound her guinea pig makes when it squeaks, you won't say, "I love that you added the *ee, ee, ee* sound to your story. I hope you add that squeaking sound into your stories often!" Instead, you'll name what the child has done in a way that makes the action replicable: "I love the way you reread and added teeny details that could help readers create movies in their minds of exactly what happened. You made it so I can hear your guinea pig. Whenever you write, add details like these." Or, "I love the way you've brought out dialogue—even if it is guinea pig dialogue! You didn't just say, 'Freddy made noises to greet me.' You told us exactly what he said!"

The best is if you can actually take in the new work that a youngster has tackled, the surprising power in his or her writing, and compliment something that represents the outer edge of the child's development. John Hattie's research suggests that compliments—what he refers to as *medals*—need to be informative. The point is not to pile on platitudes. It is to let a writer know that something he or she has been doing is really working—something the writer may not even realize he or she has been doing.

Teach and coach, reducing the scaffolding as you work together.

The teaching phase of a conference is remarkably similar to a minilesson. You'll make it clear that the conference has turned a corner and that you now want to explicitly teach the writer something that you hope will help her not only today, with this piece, but also in future writing projects. You might say

something like, "There's one tip, one very important tip, that I think will help you not only with this piece but also with future pieces. One thing I'd suggest is. . . ." Alternatively, you might say, "May I teach you one thing that I think will really, really help you a lot?" This helps the student know how to listen to what you are about to teach.

You'll word the teaching point in such a way that it can be generalized to other instances. For example, you might say, "One strategy I use when I want to do what you are doing [convince my reader, write a really effective list, angle a story so that it makes a point] is. . . ." Of course, you could refer to other writers rather than yourself: "Many writers find that to . . . it helps to. . . . Specifically, they often. . . ."

Sometimes, after offering a strategy, you can ask the writer either to go off on his or her own and try the strategy you've just described or to get started trying to do that work right now, as you watch (and coach). Often, though, you'll need to give an example from your own work or even show the writer what this might look like in her work. The point will be to use whatever you have on hand to demonstrate the step-by-step process a writer goes through to use that strategy to help him reach his goal.

Sometimes after you give a quick demonstration yourself or show a quick example, you'll want the student to try the work while you watch and coach. For example, imagine the writer of an information book has written only one sentence of information about each of her subtopics, and you've suggested that she could reread the piece and star places where she could say more, then add onto those places. In this case, you might suggest she point to places in the text where she plans to write more and say aloud what she plans to write. Or, if you decide the writer needs more support, you might say, "So let's try this together," then you could read aloud the relevant portion of the writer's draft, leaving spaces for the writer to do the new work. After helping—scaffolding—in that way, you'd note the child's progress and perhaps suggest the youngster continue this work, and meanwhile this time you can watch and provide fewer scaffolds.

The Link Phase

Soon you will need to leave the child to work independently. That is, after the writer has done a bit of the work on her or his own (even if that work occurs in the conference, with the benefit of your scaffolding), you will want to step back and name what the writer has done that that he can do again in another instance within this draft and when working on another piece of writing. "Keep going," you'll say at the end of the conference. You'll be sure to clarify the work the writer still needs to do. "Now that you have added all this information to the stuff you already wrote, do you think that when you write new things, you could write more about each thing? Maybe you could have one page be about one subtopic, the next page about the next subtopic . . . ?" As part of this, it is not uncommon for you to repeat the teaching point, this time not as a charge to the writer but as a record of what the writer has just done. As you remind the writer that it will be important to continue doing this good work often in future writing pieces, you'll explicitly support transference of what you have taught today into the child's ongoing independent writing process.

The challenge is to do all this, making sure the youngster's energy for writing goes up, not down. The single most important guideline to keep in mind in a conference is this: the writer should leave wanting to write.

When you follow the general pattern as outlined here, conferences become more manageable. There will be some writing workshops where you spend your whole time conferring, in which case you can hold half a dozen intense, meaningful teaching interactions such as these, each one tailored to the individual needs of a child. More often, you'll divide your time between conferring and small-group work, holding half as many conferences and an equal number of small-group coaching sessions. As mentioned earlier, small-group coaching sessions follow a structure similar to one-to-one conferences, with some key differences. One difference is that the research and decision phases typically happen prior to pulling the small group of writers

together. That is, you will have noticed several children struggling with a similar problem—for example, what to add and what to cut during revision—and you'll have already decided they would benefit from a small-group session. In this way, the research and decision phases happen on the run and prior to your small-group coaching. After establishing who—and what—you will teach, the teaching and link phases then follow a similar pattern to those of one-to-one conferences, though typically there is a shorter demonstration or teaching point, followed by more time for students to practice the new skill or strategy as the teacher provides lean scaffolds, quickly moving from student to student. Other types of small-group sessions center around shared writing or inquiry. The benefits of pulling a small group together for a strategy session are (1) you can maximize your instruction across three or four students, (2) observe closely as students practice the new strategy (providing lean directives as needed), and (3) remove scaffolding for children as they work toward independence.

Whether you spend most of the workshop conferring or split your time between conferring and small-group coaching sessions, the challenge is to lead effective conferences—quickly! Once you become skilled at this general template, it will allow you to channel your attention and thoughts to individual writers and to decide on and support the specific next steps each child can take.

It is tremendously important that you confer regularly with children and that you do so in ways that teach children to confer with themselves. You need to ask writers the questions that writers can profitably ask themselves. And you need, as much as possible, to hand over the conferences to the children, letting them become, with your support, both writer and reader, creator and critic.

Supporting English Language Learners

BECAUSE THE TEACHERS COLLEGE Reading and Writing Project works primarily in schools where classrooms brim with English language learners, we spend a lot of time thinking about ways the writing workshop can be adjusted so that it is especially supportive for our ELLs. In many of our schools, teachers, coaches, and administrators have been working for decades on teaching writing and teaching language simultaneously throughout the workshop.

Balancing both—teaching writing and teaching language—is challenging but greatly rewarding for students and teachers. Many of the English learners in our classrooms are eager for the challenge. As their teachers, we need to find ways to communicate and help them access the information they need to grow in their language skills and give them lots of opportunities to write and speak in both their first language and in English. Some support for English learners is embedded in the framework of the writing workshop itself.

WAYS THE WRITING WORKSHOP ALREADY SUPPORTS ELLS

Consistent Teaching Structures

Workshop classrooms are organized in such clear, predictable, consistent ways that children quickly become comfortable participating in their ongoing structures. Very early in the school year, ELL children come to understand that writing workshops start with the teacher giving a minilesson, and that during the minilesson they learn strategies that they are then expected to apply to their independent work. Children know that after the minilesson they will be expected to write independently and that the teacher will circulate around the room, conferring with individuals and with small groups. Children also know that they will be expected at some point to share their work with a partner. When the writing time is over, children know that they need to put their materials away and gather

A GUIDE TO THE COMMON CORE WRITING WORKSHOP, INTERMEDIATE GRADES in the meeting area (or with a partner) for a share session. When teachers follow these routines day after day, students can focus their energies on trying to figure out how to do their work rather than on worrying over what they will be expected to do. The predictability of the workshop provides tremendous reassurance to a child who is just learning English, and this is amplified if workshop structures repeat themselves across other subjects.

Consistent Teaching Language

In addition, writing workshops are characterized by a consistent instructional language. The consistency of this language scaffolds each child's classroom experience, making it easier for a child who is just learning English to grasp the unique content that is being taught that day. For example, it helps that most minilessons start in a predictable manner, with teachers saying, "Writers," and then reviewing the content of previous minilessons, perhaps referencing a bulleted entry on a class chart. It helps children that every day the teacher encapsulates the day's minilesson in a sentence or two (the teaching point), which is repeated often and usually written down on a chart.

Plentiful Opportunities for Writing Practice

Of course, the predictability of the workshop also means that teachers needn't invent a new way each day to support English language learners. Because the same classroom structures are in place day after day, solutions that help on Tuesday will also help on Wednesday, Thursday, and Friday. This level of consistency, as well as predictability of activity and language, gives language learners not only a space for learning language but a place to practice. Whether your English language learner is a beginning speaker or an advanced one, she will have the opportunity to work on her writing and language skills each day. Repetition and practice are two important scaffolds that English language learners need to grow their literacy skills. They need to expand both their receptive language skills—their listening and reading—as well as their expressive language skills—their speaking and writing. The writing workshop is one more place where both of these skills can be cultivated.

Differentiation through Choice and Social Interaction

Then, too, the work that children do in the writing workshop continually, inevitably, provides wonderful learning opportunities for English language learners. Because the child always chooses what she will write about, chooses the words she will use, chooses the people and places and topics and opinions that will be brought forth in the texts, chooses meanings that are vibrantly important to her, chooses the level of vocabulary and of sentence and text structures, and so forth, the writing workshop is *by definition* always individualized.

Here is the really powerful thing about the writing workshop: by definition, it's also utterly *interpersonal*. Try it. Write about the things that are on your mind. Put your mom on the page or your son; capture that memory that haunts you or the topic you're an expert on; convince others that the cause or issue you are passionate about is worth their attention. Now bring this page to the table when you gather with the people who live and work alongside you. Share the text. Talk about it. You will find that by sharing your writing, something happens that makes you and the people with whom you live and work see one another in a new way; sometimes it will almost seem as if you are seeing one another for the first time. You will see that if you share your writing with your colleagues, you will go through each school day with a different sense of yourself and your workplace, and the same will be true for your ELLs. You'll understand the song, "No Man Is an Island," and its message that no one is alone, and we all share each others' joys and griefs. For every one of us, the chance to work and learn in the presence of a community of others is invaluable. Could we possibly give anything more precious to our English language learners? To all of our children?

Contextualized Exposure to New Genres, Structures, and Vocabularies

As students begin to write and think about their own stories, information texts, and persuasive essays, they will be given the opportunity over and over again to learn new vocabulary, use new language structures, and work on expressing their thoughts in a highly contextualized and pertinent situation. That is to say, they will be learning about language in a culturally relevant and high-interest activity and writing about material that comes from their own lives and experiences.

USING ASSESSMENT TO TAILOR THE WORKSHOP TO PROVIDE EXTRA SUPPORT FOR ELLS IN ALL STAGES OF LEARNING ENGLISH

Of course, there is no such thing as *the* English language learner. Language learners, like all learners, differ one from the next in a host of ways. Two significant factors contributing to their unique needs are the child's level of competence in his or her first language and the child's English proficiency.

Knowing where each student is in his or her English acquisition allows you to plan minilessons, confer with students, and set up supportive partnerships more strategically. Assessing your students' language proficiency, just as you assess their writing skills, is important to do so you can identify goals and expectations that you will help them work toward in writing workshop. Ninety percent of the language we have is acquired over time. So knowing what areas of language your ELLs know—for example, conversational English versus academic English—will help you coach your students during writing time. For language they don't know yet, you can create partnerships where they will hear those parts of language in context, and you can use those parts of language with kids during conferring and small-group sessions. Identifying language that kids use but confuse can help you identify goals that you can work on with kids, encouraging them to use those words with more effectiveness in their writing.

Most school districts have a language assessment, but every day in the writing workshop you are able to collect language samples, both written and oral. The more you look at the student and the language she uses throughout the day, in different contexts, the more you will be able to identify and support her in where she needs to move next linguistically.

It's critical that you think through how each of the components of a writing workshop can be altered to provide ELLs with the support they need. Most language learners go through predictable stages of language acquisition as they move to full fluency in English. When you plan the writing workshop, you need to think about how you are going to meet your children's needs as they develop English language skills and how you are going to adjust your expectations while children are moving toward full fluency. But let us think now about specific ways each of the components of the writing workshop can be altered just a bit so that the workshop as a whole is especially supportive for ELLs.

Support in the Preproduction and Early Production Stages of Learning English

When students are in the first few stages of language acquisition they are generally working on learning such things as common nouns, prepositions, pronouns, and present tense.

Make your teaching and the words you use (students' words as well) as clear as possible.

You will want to help students build language by exposing them to language they can understand. What are some ways that you can make your teaching and talk more comprehensible to students?

- Use a lot of *visual examples in your teaching*. A teacher might, for example, have in her demonstration piece a picture that shows the small moment she is writing about or an image that captures some of the information she is including in her piece. Sometimes I see teachers using their whole body when teaching a lesson, becoming highly animated. This is not only because animated teaching can grab and take hold of their students' attention but also because doing so makes their teaching and language more comprehensible. These teachers use gestures, facial expressions, and intonation. In other words, they dramatize their teaching and talk to help make it more comprehensible.

- Offer students the use of *visual examples in their own writing*. In the beginning stages of language acquisition, whether working in English or their first language, students need to use pictures alongside their writing. This way the teacher or the child's partner has something recognizable to talk about with him or her. Also, this allows students to write about things they do not necessarily have the vocabulary for yet. Pictures give the teacher as well as the community ways to know what the child is writing about and help aid communication between teacher and student.

Provide opportunities for listening and for learning the social language of the writing workshop.

Children who are in the silent period (preproduction stage) or in the early production stages of learning English will have few oral English skills, but they will be listening carefully, trying to interpret what is going on around them. It is okay for children to be quiet at this stage, but it is important to understand that they are taking in a lot of information. The English words, phrases, and sentences that will make sense to them first will probably be the predictable sentences related to concrete classroom activities, such as "Get your writing," "Draw something on this paper," "You can go to your seat now," or "Let's gather in the meeting area."

Opportunities for listening, really listening, are important, and the expectation that these children will participate in the comings and goings of the class spotlights the importance of them learning the social language that is most within their grasp. It is important that these children *are* being told, "Get out your pencil," "Draw here," and "Let's gather in the meeting area" (with accompanying gestures) and that they are expected to do all these things along with the others.

Establish partnerships and triads that support ELLs' burgeoning language development.

The writing workshop is an especially rich context for language development because children are not only writing and listening; they are also talking—and much of that talk happens in the small, supportive structures of partnerships. Eventually, these partnerships will give children important opportunities to rehearse for writing, but when children are in the preproduction stage of learning English, a partnership with one other child could make the child at the early production stage feel trapped, like a deer in the headlights, with nowhere to hide. Still, it is crucial that new arrivals are expected to join into the class as best they can right from the start. There is never a time when new arrivals sit on the edge of the community, watching. Instead, the rug spot for the new arrival needs to be right in the center of the meeting area, and from the start, when children turn and talk during the active engagement section of a minilesson, these children must know that they belong to a conversational group.

Children in the early stages of learning English benefit from being in triads, not partnerships; ideally one child in that triad will share the new arrival's native language but be more proficient in English, and the other child will be a native speaker of English (and a language model).

Granted, children who are in the preproduction stage of learning English will mostly listen. You can teach their more English-proficient partners how to use lots of gestures and to ask the child questions that can be answered with a yes or a no, a nod or a head shake.

You will want to coach your kids on how to work together in various configurations in the classroom. Many students benefit from meeting often with a peer to read their piece or talk about what it is that they have written and to get feedback on their writing. These conversations not only give them valuable feedback, but they also create opportunities for comprehensible language input from a peer. Many students in the first few stages of language acquisition also benefit from working with a partner to help them rehearse what they are going to write. Oral language rehearsal and practicing the words out loud is a wonderful strategy to help kids "work out" and test what they want to write. So often for our students, it takes a couple of times to think about how it might go on the page to help them find exactly what they want to say and how to say it. This is a good use of partner time in both the upper-grade and lower-grade classrooms.

> "The writing workshop is an especially rich context for language development because children are also talking, often in the small, supportive structures of partnerships."

Provide your ELLs opportunities to write in both their first language and in English.

When a child in the first stages of acquiring English arrives in a classroom, the first goal is to make sure that child is immediately active and interactive. If this child is literate in his or her first language, then by all means it is important for the child to write (and to read) in that language. If there are people in the classroom or the school who can speak the child's native language, you can rely on this buddy to convey to the child the kind of text that the class is writing and some of the main qualities of that type of writing. For example, this buddy might convey, "We are writing about our opinions, about changes we want to see in our school or community, and a few reasons why."

Whether or not the new arrival is literate in his first language, you will want that child to write as best he can in his first language while also offering him opportunities to begin doing some writing in English. Some teachers find that it helps for these children to have time slots for first-language writing and for English writing, with the child perhaps starting the writing workshop with fifteen minutes to write in his first language. (During this time, the child can write with volume that is comparable to other children and build his identity as a child who writes a lot.) But it is also important for this child to write in English.

Usually we start by asking the child who is in the early stages of learning English to draw and label her drawing when writing in English. This, of course, is reminiscent of what we ask kindergarten and first-grade children to do. There is nothing "elementary" about learning a second language, and yet taking children new to English through the progression of work that younger children in a writing workshop experience has all sorts of advantages. After a child has drawn and labeled in English for a bit, you can ask the child to start writing in sentences. These children need the same range of paper choices that you normally offer children in earlier grades. It is especially important that these children have access to paper that contains a large box at the top of the page, and several lines for writing under that box. The size of the box shrinks and the number of lines increases as children develop proficiency in English. This progression of paper choice is an extremely powerful way to scaffold children's language development. Imagine that the child has written about a soccer game in her first language and drawn a series of sketches showing what happened first, next, and last in the game. Then, with help from English-speaking peers, the child labels each drawing with lots of English words, providing herself with a picture dictionary that is tailored to her exact story. It is not such a big step, then, to ask this child to use those words and write a sentence or two to accompany each of her drawings.

Plan instruction with your ESL instructor to maximize learning in the writing workshop.

If you have children who are in the early stages of English acquisition, it is especially important to provide them with extra help understanding the content of a minilesson. If there is an English as a second language teacher who is willing to provide support, this can also be extremely beneficial. Some ESL teachers "push in" to classrooms; some ESL teachers "pull out" children for work in the ESL room. While not always possible, we recommend that ELLs remain in the classroom to maximize interaction and instructional opportunities. But, in either case, working in tandem with your ESL teacher will benefit your ELLs.

If classroom teachers and ESL teachers have opportunities to plan together, the ESL teacher can support the children during writing workshop by pre-teaching the concepts and developing the vocabulary necessary to understand what will be taught in the minilesson. For example, if the minilesson will teach children how to write with main ideas and support ideas, the ESL teacher might use a nonfiction content-area book and lots of gestures to convey that the title of the book is the main idea or the big idea, and then to convey that some of the subtitles are support ideas (or smaller ideas). The teacher could reinforce the concept of ordination and subordination (without using those terms) by showing that if the classroom represents a big topic, the library area could represent a subtopic.

Many ESL teachers will also work with groups of students to help target specific parts of language. They may use shared writing or interactive writing as a way to build language structures that relate to the unit of study that students are in. Many teachers also then conduct group conferences with students who are working on the same parts of language.

Create concise minilessons that rely on visuals and familiar references.

There are other ways to alter minilessons to support English language learners. First, you will want your minilessons to be as concise as possible. If you are working with a large ELL population, you'll want to trim the minilessons in this series! Then, too, visuals can make a huge difference. It helps to draw and act as you talk. Sketch almost any story, information book, or persuasive text as you tell it. If you want to describe the way a writer can "stretch out" sections of a story, for example, it helps to tug on the ends of a rubber band whenever saying the term *stretch out*. You will also probably make a special point of using examples that children can relate to. It's helpful to repeat the teaching point more often with children who are learning English. Similarly, when you want children to turn and talk, it can help set them up with cue cards. In an essay unit, for example, you might give them cards that say "one example . . ." "another example . . . ," and so forth.

Plan a double active engagement section of your minilesson.

Some teachers find that if they've used writing-in-the-air to demonstrate something and want children to learn from their example, children profit from first retelling the teacher's version of the text before they then apply these principles to their own piece. This leads some teachers to set up a double active engagement within many minilessons.

Support in the Later Stages of Learning English

It is important to celebrate the work that children at this stage of early emergent English are producing, focusing on the content and quality of their spoken and written texts, not only on the correctness of the syntax. These children are taking risks, and your job is to help them to feel successful.

Move students in this stage from triads to partnerships or pair them with an early emergent ELL.

As children begin to acquire more fluency in English, they will be able to understand written and spoken English when they have concrete contexts (pictures, actions, sounds, and so on). As they develop these proficiencies, you might move them from triads to partnerships (or nudge them to become one of the more vocal members of a triad, with a new preproduction ELL joining in as best as he or she can). You know these learners will not always use correct syntax, but also know they can participate fully in partnership work. Remember that all language learners need the best language models possible. So keep this in mind as you determine your partnerships and triads.

Extend the language ELLs are producing.

As children become more proficient in English, their answers to questions will become more extended, even though their hold on English grammar and vocabulary will still be approximate. Again, partners (and teachers) can be coached to realize that this is not a time for correcting grammar. Instead, it is a time for expanding on what the child says. If the child points to a picture she has drawn as part of a story she's written and says, "Mom," then you'll want to expand on this. "That's your mom?" *Pause for a nod.* "You and your Mom," *pointing*, "went in the car?" *Point again.* "Where did you go?" *Gesture to illustrate that the question pertains to where the car drove.* If the child isn't

sure how to answer, you can eventually supply options, "Did you go to the store? Or to the park?"

Scaffold children's writing with conversational prompts.

To help children bring a growing repertoire of language from the minilessons into their independent work, you might scaffold the writing that children do (and also the conversations that children have during work time with their partners) by providing them with conversational prompts. For example, in an opinion unit, you might teach children to write or say, "I see . . ." and then to shift and write or say, "I think. . . ." The thought can be elaborated on when the child learns transition phrases such as "for example. . . ." Children who are just learning English may rely heavily on these prompts, and you may even write cue cards for them.

Provide time for in-context grammar instruction.

While it is important to support children's attempts at emerging syntax, children also need instruction. For example, if children are writing personal narratives, you might teach and then post transition words that show that a little time has passed, such as *then*, *later*, *after a while*, *five minutes later*, or *next*. You might remind children that in their stories or essays, as they move from one moment in time to the next, they will often use a transition word to show that time has passed. To practice this, you might ask one partner to tell another what he or she did since walking into the classroom, remembering to insert words that show the passage of time. When partners meet, you can suggest that they talk through the sequence of events in each child's writing, using transition words as the storyteller or essayist progresses from one moment in time to the next. Each child will also benefit from having a list of these transition words during work time.

Support in Learning Academic English

As important as it is for you to tailor work time during the writing workshop so that children in the early stages of English acquisition receive the help they need, it is equally important for you to be cognizant that children who are in later stages of language acquisition also need special support. When children reach intermediate fluency, they demonstrate increased levels of accuracy and are able to express their thoughts and feelings in English. They often sound as if their English is stronger than it is. This is because though these children may have developed conversational skills, often they still do not have academic English language skills. These children have a strong command of social English and can use English to chat with each other, to learn what the teacher expects them to do, and to talk about the events of the day. They may sound "fluent" in social conversation where complex structures can be avoided, but it is often difficult to follow them when they describe events from another time and place.

One way to determine whether a child needs help with academic English is to talk to the child about a story in a novel or about something that happened in another time and place. Invite the child to retell an episode from the book or from the child's experience; listen well. If the child's language is such that you have a hard time piecing together what she is trying to say, chances are good this child needs support with academic English. The term *academic English* does not refer only to the language that is used in discipline-based studies. It refers to the language that a person must use to communicate about times and places that are distant and unfamiliar and that must be created by words.

The challenge for these children is that they now need to learn academic English; to do this, they need input from people who can provide strong language models and from skilled teachers.

Scaffold students' work on elaboration and writing with description and specificity.

At this stage it is very important for teachers to work on elaboration and specificity to help children use more descriptive and extended language. It is also important for these children to be partnered with children for whom English is their first language, children who can function as strong language models. Often, when teachers have a handful of children who are in the earliest stages of language acquisition and a handful who are further along, teachers devote most of their special attention to the children who are the newest to English. However, if you set new arrivals up with the proper invitations to work, support structures from other children, and ways of being interactive, they can learn a huge amount from each other. Meanwhile, you can devote your time to children who have a good command of social English but not of academic English and need help that is less readily available from the peer group.

Provide explicit instruction in tenses, pronoun references, connectors, and so on.

Children who need help with academic English will profit from explicit instruction tailored to their needs. For example, these children benefit from instruction in connectives. They tend to write in simple sentences, linked together with the connector *and*. It is important for children to study connectors, because when English language learners learn to read as well as to write, these can become a source of confusion. Many readers assume that sentences are arranged in chronological order. However, in many sentences, that assumption is incorrect; for example, "I went to the office because the principal called for me over the PA system." In small-group instruction, then, you will want to provide English language learners with explicit instruction to help them understand connectors, tenses, pronoun references, and so forth.

Support students in building vocabulary using their own writing as the context.

Of course, English language learners also need support in developing a rich vocabulary, and again, these children benefit from explicit instruction. If a child overuses a word such as *nice* or *beautiful*, you will want to help him learn that there are many different, more precise words the child could use. Is the person lovely? Impressive? Unusual? Dignified? Cute? Some teachers help children to develop word files, with the overused word at the center of a card and five variations of that word around the edges. Children keep these cards on hand throughout the day and look for opportunities to use specific words orally (some teachers ask children to place a check mark beside a word each time they use it orally).

This word bank should also be on hand when the child writes. If a child decides that her beloved mother is not dignified but cute, then the child's personal connection to the word will make it more memorable than had the child merely encountered it in a class on vocabulary.

Similarly, if children are writing about a particular subject, the teacher or an English-speaking buddy may want to help the child build a domain-specific vocabulary to draw upon as he or she writes. If the child is writing about attending a carnival, she would benefit from having a conversation about her experience at the carnival. This sort of rehearsal is important to every writer, but it can provide an extra language support to the English language learner who is ready to learn precise vocabulary.

Provide small-group instruction for students to learn figurative language.

Children learning academic English will also need support as they come to understand and use figurative language. Of course, literature is filled with metaphors and similes, as are the minilessons in this series. Children who are just on the brink of learning academic English will profit from some small-group instruction that gives them access to literary devices.

YOUR TEACHING IN EVERY UNIT CAN SUPPORT WRITING GOALS—AND LANGUAGE GOALS

When you approach a unit of study, you need to think about the language needs of ELL children in the classroom: what are the language skills that your children need to have to understand the work they are being asked to do? You need to think not only about the writing skills and strategies that will be developed in a unit but also about the language skills the unit will support. You need to think about the vocabulary, the idiomatic expressions, the connectives, the conjunctions, and the grammar you want children to develop in a unit. There has to be a plan for content and a plan for language, side by side.

When approaching a unit on information writing, for example, you can anticipate that you'll be teaching children how to explain, describe, compare, categorize, and question. It's likely that you'll mostly be helping children write in present tense and that they'll benefit from learning connectives such as *if*, *when*, *because*, *for example*, *another example*, and so forth. You can plan that you might provide scaffolds such as a chart of phrases, and you can know in advance that children may need help with instructional terms such as *fact*, *example*, *type*, *reason*, and *description*. You know you may teach the language of comparison, including, for example, the use of the *-er* and *-est* word endings, as in *big*, *bigger*, *biggest*.

The power of written curriculum is that you and a group of colleagues can hold your hopes for teaching in your hands and talk and think together about how you can take your own best ideas and make them better. One of the most important ways to make your teaching stronger is to think, How can we give all children access to this teaching? The wonderful thing about a workshop is that it is incredibly supportive for English language learners, but if you bring your best ideas to the table, you can make the writing workshop even more supportive.

Chapter 10

Building Your Own
Units of Study

I F THIS SERIES HAS DONE ITS JOB WELL it will not only have helped you to *teach the units* described to good effect, but it also will have encouraged you to work collaboratively with your colleagues to *author your own units of study*. In their new book, *Professional Capital*, Michael Fullan and Andy Hargreaves (2012) point out that master teachers not only study and learn *best* practices; they also have the skills, the knowledge, and the confidence to develop the *next* practices. This series has been carefully constructed with an eye toward teaching you to author your own units of study in writing.

In this chapter, I pass along what I've learned about the process of developing curriculum in hopes that this can help you and your colleagues create units of study to fill gaps that we have left in the curriculum. You'll want to be in a position to respond to priorities in your region, and to your students' interests and your own, by authoring units that aren't described in Units of Study in Opinion, Information, and Narrative Writing. The book *If . . . Then . . . Curriculum: Assessment-Based Instruction* will help you imagine some possible units, suggesting broad contours for them, and I hope some of these units appeal to you so that our unit summaries can function as a scaffold, supporting you as you develop your own writing curriculum. But I also know that you will want to develop your own units of study from scratch; this chapter can help you do that.

DECIDE ON THE SUBJECT FOR YOUR UNIT OF STUDY

First, you will need to decide on what it is you will teach. You will see that the units that we've detailed in this series tend to be genre based; genre is one of the great organizers of writing. Genre is a rather obvious way to organize students' work with writing. It is easier to imagine planning a unit of study on a kind of writing—whether that writing consists of op-ed columns or how-to books—than on a part of the writing process or a quality of good writing because units on a particular genre will inevitably encompass the full span of the writing process. In a genre study, students begin to imagine what they will be writing by doing some reading. Then they rehearse, draft, revise, and edit that kind of writing—either progressing through one cycle or through many cycles of writing, producing one finished text or many. Certainly there are many genres that have not been addressed in the current series. Some of these—such as historical fiction, journalism, and fantasy—have been sketched out in *If . . . Then . . . Curriculum*, but many others remain as wide open terrain.

But it is also important for you to understand that you can design units of study that are not genre based. For example, you could design a unit of study on revision, channeling students to review their folders full of writing and to select several pieces from throughout the year that deserve to be revised, then helping them set to work with those pieces of writing. In a similar way, you could conceivably design a unit of study on a topic such as author studies. This, like a unit on revision, could involve students revising pieces they wrote earlier in the year, but this time doing so under the influence of authors. Alternatively, you could develop a unit focusing on a quality of good writing. For example, you could rally children to closely study places where authors "show, not tell." Children could then revise their existing texts to show, not tell, more often, and eventually they could draft new texts, using all they've learned. There are other qualities of good writing I could imagine studying: characterization, for example, or the development of reasons and evidence to support a thesis statement.

Then, too, you could study a social structure that supports writing. For example, you could design a unit of study called "Writing Friendships," in which you help children consider how to work well with a partner and perhaps with a writing club. How might a writing partnership best help with rehearsal for writing? With drafting? With revision?

Although it is possible to design units of study on topics such as these rather than on genre, these topics will be more challenging. If you have experience developing units of study for writing, have a mentor working closely with you, or if you are following one of the plans laid out in your grade's *If . . . Then . . . Curriculum* book, you might decide to try your hand at such a unit. In the absence of these supports, I suggest you may want to start by developing a genre-based unit of study.

In any case, take some time to mull over possible topics for the unit, guarding against the temptation to seize on the first topic of study that comes to mind.

Clarify your goals by thinking about what unit of study would especially benefit your children, keeping in mind what they can do and can almost do.

When you decide on a unit of study, you are taking it on yourself to channel the young people in your care to devote at least a month of their writing lives toward the topic that you settle on. Therefore, it is important to weigh whether a particular topic will be especially beneficial for children. When a unit of study comes to mind, you'll want to put it through the test of asking a few hard questions. Start by asking, "Will the skills students develop during this unit of study be important ones for them? Will the unit be a high-leverage one, setting youngsters up to do similar work in other genres or in other areas of the curriculum?" For example, a teacher decides that she wants her children to become more skilled at writing proficient first-draft writing on demand. For this reason, she may decide to turn the classroom into a newsroom and teach children to write news articles and editorials. That decision makes sense.

It goes without saying that you need to believe any unit of study that you teach (or any unit you impose on your children) must be incredibly important. You probably won't want to channel all of your students to spend a month or six weeks of time working on a genre that doesn't seem to you as if it will provide students with skills that will be foundational or transferable. For example, a unit on limericks or sea shanties or haiku might be fun, but before embarking on such a unit, I'd want to weigh whether it would pay off as much as other units.

Then, too, think about how the unit relates to your students' skill levels in relation to standards for their grade and to their zone of proximal development. As you think about this, you'll find yourself honing in on what, exactly, you will be teaching within the topic. For example, one could teach a unit on investigative journalism that reminded students of what they already know about the structure of information writing and that focused especially on

> *"Take some time to mull over possible topics for a unit; your students will devote at least a month of their writing lives to it."*

research—on collecting and integrating information from a wide variety of sources and synthesizing that information into coherent texts. Alternatively, a unit on investigative journalism could help students write what they already know—about events in school, home, and their community—with an emphasis on the essentials of information writing. In the same way, if you were to teach a unit on revision, the decision to address that topic wouldn't, alone, provide a clear direction for your unit. Do you want to focus on students writing to discover new insights or on the physical tools for (and reasons for) adding and subtracting to a text and the challenges of elaboration? Of course, you could select an entirely different focus altogether for a unit on revision. My point only is that once you decide on the terrain for the unit of study you will teach, you still need to hone in on specific skills, and to do that, you need to know your students well and to think hard about their entire writing curriculum.

For example, if you and your colleagues decided to develop a unit of study on poetry, you'd want to think about how that unit would fit into earlier and later work across students' school careers on poetry—and on writing in general. You would want to take some time to create a gradient of difficulty for studying poetry. What might be more accessible for younger writers? More demanding for older writers? You might, for example, decide that for more novice writers, a unit on poetry could highlight reading-writing connections and revision, and for more proficient writers, a unit on poetry could highlight imagery and metaphor. Of course, both reading-writing connections and metaphor can be taught in simpler or more complex ways, so you and your colleagues might decide instead to study imagery and metaphor across the grades, with increasing levels of sophistication and challenge.

Here is a final word about one's choice of a unit of study: the other deciding factor is *you*. If you are learning to play the guitar and find yourself dying for the chance to dig into song writing, then consider bringing that passion into the classroom. If you loved teaching your fiction unit and yearn to do more, consider a unit on revision or on character development (which could invite children to revise several earlier pieces to bring the characters more to life) or historical fiction. In the end, children can grow as writers within any unit of study. And whether you are teaching a unit on independence in the writing workshop or on writing to change the world, you need to remember in particular that you are teaching children, and teaching writing. The rest is negotiable.

PLAN THE WORK CHILDREN WILL DO

It is tempting to start planning a unit of study by writing a minilesson for Day One and then for Day Two. What I have found is that if I proceed in that manner, chances are greater that those intricate, time-consuming plans will end up being jettisoned.

I recommend instead that you begin by thinking about the work that you envision your children doing in this unit. For example, before you can imagine the unit's flow, you need to decide whether children will be writing one piece during the unit or two or many. Assuming children are cycling through the writing process more than once, writing more than one text, will they work the whole time on one kind of writing, or will they start with one kind of writing before switching to another kind? For example, in one unit students begin by writing information chapter books and end by writing feature articles; in another they begin by writing persuasive speeches and end by writing petitions and letters. Also, you need to decide whether writers will proceed in synchronization with one another or whether some children will write three texts and some only one. Then, too, you need to decide whether you imagine children progressing quickly through rehearsal, spending more time on revision, or vice versa.

We always spend a lot of time constructing a storyline through the unit, one that orients the bends in the road of the unit. The storyline for the fourth-grade personal and persuasive essays, for example, proceeds as follows. This is a new genre for students, so we begin by putting them all into an intensive shared experience of essay writing. Over the course of a day or two, all students participate in what we refer to as "essay boot camp." During that time, all students fast-write a very quick essay that is structured in the simplest, most traditional fashion possible—but is nonetheless structured. Then the next phase of the unit begins. Students learn to live like essayists, collecting the grist for personal essays and growing ideas in their writer's notebooks. Those ideas might be written as rough essays, or they may be written as freewriting. Then writers are brought step by step through a detailed process of writing an essay before they are released and encouraged to write another essay, this time a persuasive essay, and this time, written while on their own.

When planning the work that students will do, it is important to think about the progression of endeavors that they might possibly take on, choosing work that will be challenging for the class but not so challenging that they are brought to a halt. For example, when considering how to help students write research reports on the American Revolution, we knew that the unit would be a challenging one. Students would be writing about content they probably didn't have a real strong handle on, and they'd be wrestling with sources and domain-specific vocabulary in ways that would be challenging. And what, really, could we reasonably expect them to write early on in the unit?

We decided to first channel children to write little four-page booklets containing a few chapters that we figured would be especially accessible for them. We suggested that one page of the booklets might be an all-about summary of the American Revolution, another page, an all-about summary of the event each writer selected (for example, the Boston Tea Party). Those two pages would require similar writing work, and in neither instance would students be expected to elaborate on focused topics in ways that would be especially difficult. Next we imagined that students might write a "Day in the Life of . . ." narrative and a "This is important because . . ." essay. We wanted to first give students a goal that we knew would be doable for them. We knew, too, that by the time students met that goal, they'd be ready for a new and more challenging one. This next goal, of course, required more choice as well as more complexity. Students were ready to handle those challenges because they stood on the stairway of the earlier work.

It helps to imagine different ways that the unit of study you've selected might proceed and then weigh the pros and cons of those various alternatives. Whatever the genre, whatever the form, there are some principles that underlie the progressions in most units. Early in the unit, students generally work with synchronicity to complete one or sometimes two pieces of writing. During this phase, we do a lot of instruction, and that teaching is captured on anchor charts. Then in most units, we ask students to transfer what they have just learned to the work they do writing a new text. They work on the new text with new levels of independence, and they not only apply all they've learned during the first portion of the unit, but they also stand on the shoulders of that early work to reach for more demanding goals.

These are a few common templates, then, for a unit of study:

- Your children might generate lots of one kind of writing, perhaps taking each bit of writing through a somewhat limited amount of revision. Then your children look back over all of that writing to choose one piece (presumably from the writing they've only lightly revised) to delve into with more depth, bringing it to completion. After this, students work on the entire cycle of writing, this time working under the influence of a mentor text, aiming to do all they did previously, only better now, as they emulate published work.

- Your children may start with an intensive, two-day immersion into the kind of writing they will be doing in the unit, doing this work with lots of support from you. Then all the members of the class work in synchronism on their own writing projects. This project contains lots of parts or steps, and you coach writers along each step (or aspect) of the piece. After completing that one main project, students fast-draft a quicker version of that project.

Let's imagine that you decide to teach a unit on poetry. You'd probably find this fits best into the first template. Presumably, at the start of the unit each child could write and lightly revise a bunch of poems. Then writers could commit themselves to taking one poem (or a collection of poems that address one topic) through more extensive revision and editing. They could then work through a similar cycle, perhaps this time writing a poetic picture book, not a poem. A unit of study on news articles could fit into that same template. News stories are written quickly, so children could generate many of these at the start of the unit, bringing more and more knowledge to them as they continue to learn more. Then you could explain that sometimes a writer decides to expand the news article into a more developed sort of writing, and you could teach children to rewrite one of their articles as an investigative report or an editorial (either project would require more research and revision).

On the other hand, you might decide that within one unit, children will work on a single, large writing project, say a piece of literary nonfiction, one requiring research. Perhaps for this unit, each child will investigate a different endangered species. You may decide that the first half of the unit will focus not on drafting information writing but on note-taking. Then, during the second half of the unit, children could draft their literary nonfiction. The unit might end with you teaching writers that the work they do when writing feature articles is not unlike the work of writing literary nonfiction books, and with all children working on a quick cycle to write feature articles.

My larger point is that before I write a single minilesson, I pull out a blank calendar for the unit and plan how the children's work is likely to unfold across the month or six weeks. If I imagine that for the first week or week-and-a-half in a unit, children will gather entries, I mark those days on the calendar. I do not yet know the specific minilessons I will teach, but I do know the broad picture of what children will be doing during those days. Proceeding in a similar fashion, I mark off the bends in the road of a unit. Even after this, however, I'm still not ready to write minilessons.

GATHER AND STUDY TEXTS FOR CHILDREN TO EMULATE

Before embarking on writing the minilessons in a unit of study, I gather and select between examples of the sort of texts I hope children will write. That is, if you decide to teach a unit on writing editorials and to emphasize the importance of the counterargument, you'll want to turn your classroom library upside down looking for examples of the sort of thing you plan to teach. You'll become a magnet for this sort of writing and find examples of it throughout your life. You will very likely want to invite your children to join you in this search, depending on where they are in their writing and reading lives at the time.

Soon you will have gathered a pile of writing, and you can begin to sift and sort through it, thinking:

- What are the different categories of texts here?
- What are the defining features of this sort of writing?
- Which of these texts could become exemplars for the unit of study?

To make these decisions, you'll need to think not only about the texts but also about your kids and about the standards that your school has adopted. You

will want to aim toward goals that are achievable for your students, and you will also want to be sure that over the course of the school year, your students meet the standards your school has adopted. For me, this means teaching in ways that are aligned to the Common Core State Standards.

Although I often gather a small stack of relevant texts, I generally select just two or perhaps three to use with children during any one unit of study. To decide on the texts that you will use as exemplars, you'll need to take into consideration the particular focus you will bring to this unit. For example, when I taught children to write fiction, I knew that I wanted their stories to involve just two or three characters and to take place across just two or three small moments. I knew, also, that I wanted the fiction to be realistic fiction. Fiction comes in all shapes and sizes, so I needed to do some research before settling on *Fireflies!* and *Pecan Pie Baby*.

Often, you will decide to use your own writing as one of the touchstone texts for the class, and you might also decide to use writing done by another child from another year. These are perfectly reasonable choices. When teaching students to write personal essays, literary essays, or research-based argument essays, it is unlikely that you'll find published work closely resembling the work you expect children to produce, so your own writing will become especially important in such instances.

When teaching, it is important to have more than one text to weave through minilessons. In the fourth-grade essay unit, for example, I often demonstrated by referencing an essay about my father, but at the same time, during the active engagement section of many minilessons, I set children up to practice what I'd demonstrated by channeling them to work on a class essay. Before you begin a unit of study, then, you may want to consider not only what the exemplar texts will be that thread throughout the unit, but also whether kids will work collaboratively on a class text.

READ, WRITE, AND STUDY WHAT YOU WILL TEACH

I describe units as if they are courses of study for children, but the truth is they are also courses for us! In addition to collecting examples of the sort of writing you'll be asking kids to do, you will also want to scoop up all the professional books and articles you can find pertaining to your unit of study. You can learn a lot from books for adult writers, so don't limit yourself to books by and for teachers.

I cannot stress enough that you also need to do the writing that you are asking your kids to do. You needn't devote a lot of time to this. The writing that you use as an exemplar text needs to be very brief anyhow, so even ten minutes of writing, four times a week, will give you tons of material to bring into your minilessons. The important thing is that during those ten minutes you work in very strategic ways. Usually you'll begin with a bare-bones small text, and you'll develop or revise it in exactly the same ways that you suggest your kids try.

As you read and write, try to think about ways in which the current unit of study could build on previous learning. Not everything that you and your kids do in this unit can be brand-new. What is it that kids already know that they can call on within this unit? What will the new work be?

Think, also, about what is essential in the unit and what is more detailed work. The answer to that question lies not only in the unit itself but in your hopes for how this unit of study will help your kids develop as writers. If you are teaching poetry with a hope that this will lead children toward being able to engage in much more extensive revision, then this goal influences your decision about what is essential in the unit.

OUTLINE A SEQUENCE OF TEACHING POINTS

After all this preparation, it will finally be time to outline a sequence of teaching points. When I do this, I am usually not totally sure which teaching points will become minilessons and which will become mid-workshop teaching points or share sessions. Those decisions often come very late, as I revise my unit.

You will want to make your plans within general time constraints. For example, I might say to myself, I will use about three days for teaching kids to highlight the central ideas in their information writing. You'll approach a set of days, then, feeling sure about the most important skills that you want to teach, and the most important content you want to convey. Then you'll decide on strategies that will help students be able to do this work. For example, in this instance, I decided that to help students highlight the central ideas in their information writing, I should teach them to reread their writing, looking

for the ideas they want to especially highlight, to stretch out the parts of their writing related to those ideas, to use introductory sentences and topic sentences to highlight those ideas, and to use text features in ways that accentuate the shared ideas. In this way, I had that progression of teaching in mind before beginning to write specific minilessons.

Before you can write minilessons, you also need to name or invent some practical, how-to procedure that you believe young writers can use to achieve a goal. For example, if I want children to use text features to highlight what a text is really about, I need to decide how to go about teaching students to do that. Maybe I'll use a mentor text to show them how another author has done it, or I'll recruit the class to work together on using text features to highlight central ideas in our class text. Once you figure out one way that youngsters can do whatever it is you want to help them to do, you are ready to teach them this strategy in a minilesson or a mid-workshop teaching point or a share.

Of course, whenever you teach anything worth teaching, you need to anticipate that kids will encounter trouble. When I teach kids ways to highlight the central ideas in information writing, for example, I need to anticipate that this will pose difficulties for some kids. At least half your teaching does not involve laying out brand-new challenges but instead involves coaching and supporting kids through predictable challenges.

> *"When you plan a unit of study, it is crucially important to foresee the difficulties kids will encounter."*

When you plan a unit of study, you'll find that it is crucially important to foresee the difficulties kids will encounter in the unit. You'll want to plan to provide students with the scaffolding necessary to succeed with first a pared-down version of what you are teaching and, eventually, with higher-level work. For example, I was pretty sure I would need to provide some scaffolding for kids when I taught them that they could reread an essay as if from a plane, looking down at the structure and the overall chunks of text. When I told kids to look at the patterns of chunks and think, What was the author doing in this chunk of text? and What about in this one? I knew that some children would find this confusing. To scaffold children's attempts to do this, I boxed out the major sections of a text I found, explaining my thinking about the work each chunk was doing. Then I asked children to try this with another text, which I'd already boxed into sections.

Although you can predict lots of the difficulties that kids will encounter as you teach them, it is inevitable that new and different issues will emerge. So you'll keep your ears attuned and your eyes alert. As you teach a unit, you'll outgrow yourself and your best teaching plans in leaps and bounds.

WRITE MINILESSONS

In writing workshops, kids generate ideas for writing, and then they select one of those to develop. They make an overall plan on either a timeline or a table of contents, or even some boxes and bullets, and then they revise those plans. They try a few alternate leads—and then get started. They write with some tentativeness, expecting to revise what they write with input from others.

The process of authoring a unit of study is not so different. You'll generate an overall plan for the unit and revise it. Eventually you'll settle on a plan and get started. After all that planning and revising, you'll write the first word. Even then, you write knowing that your teaching plans will be what Gordon Wells refers to as "an improvable object" (*Action, Talk, and Text: Learning and Teaching Through Inquiry*, 2001).

If teaching plans are only in your mind or only coded into a few words in a tiny box of a lesson-plan book, then it's not easy to revise those plans. But ever since human beings were cave dwellers, inscribing the stories of hunts on stony cave walls, we have learned that once we record our thoughts and plans, the community can gather around those thoughts. Those thoughts can be questioned, altered, and expanded. The ideas of one person can be added to the thoughts of another. In scores of schools where I work closely with teachers, we keep a binder for each unit of study. In that binder, we keep a collection of all the minilessons written that are related to each unit. Many of these are minilessons one teacher or another wrote, but others come from professional development that teachers have attended or books they've read. In these binders, the teachers also deposit other supporting material.

Hints for Writing Minilessons

The Start of the Connection

Try to think of the first part of your connection as a time to convey the reason for this minilesson. You are hoping to catch children's attention and to rally their engagement. Sometimes this is a time to step aside from writing for just a moment, telling a story or reliving a class event in a manner that will soon become a lead to (or metaphor for) whatever you will teach. Then, too, this is often a time to bring kids together to recall and apply what they have already learned that functions as a foundation for this new instruction. If you have trouble writing the start of a minilesson, it is also possible to settle for simply saying, "Yesterday I taught you . . ." and then referring to the exact words of that teaching point. These should usually be written on a chart, so gesture toward the chart as you talk. Ideally you can follow this with a memorable detail of someone who used the strategy or applied the teaching point during the preceding day's minilesson. This memorable point may be something a published author, you, or a child said or did. You can say something such as "Remember that . . . ?"

The Teaching Point

The teaching point will only be a few sentences long, but nevertheless it merits care and revision; it is the most important part of your minilesson. Plan to repeat the exact words of your teaching point at least twice in the minilesson. To learn to create teaching points, try temporarily staying within the template of these words or something very close to them: "Today, I will teach you that when writers _____, they often find it helps to _____. They do this by _____." The important thing to notice in this template is that we are not saying, "Today we will do this." A teaching point is not the assignment for the day! Instead, the teaching point is a strategy that writers often use to accomplish important writing goals. Then, too, notice that teaching points do not simply define the territory within which one will teach. That is, if a teaching point went like this, "Today I will teach you how to write good leads," then there would be nothing worth remembering in this teaching point!

The Teaching

When planning how the teaching will go, begin by deciding what your method and materials will be. If you will be demonstrating using your own writing, go back and look at a few minilessons in which I used a similar method, and at first follow the template of these minilessons. You will probably see that I set children up to participate or to observe. Then I either tell the story of how I came to need the strategy, and act out what one does first and next in using this strategy. Or, I recruit youngsters to join me in trying to use the strategy, and once they are participating, I do my work in ways that allow them to watch what I do and compare my work to what they were en route to doing. I often include in my demonstration an instance when I do something unhelpful, and then I correct myself, coming back on track. Throughout the demonstration, I tend to write only about four sentences; usually these are added to an ongoing piece that threads its way through much of the unit.

I might demonstrate using a bit of a published author's text instead of my own writing; again, if you decide to create a minilesson using that method, find instances when I did this and let them serve as an exemplar for you. You'll find that if I am demonstrating using a published author's text, I'll enact what the author probably did, prefacing my enactment with a phrase like "So and so probably did this. He probably. . . ."

I might choose not to demonstrate. Instead, for example, I might explain something and then show an example. These kinds of minilessons are more challenging to write, but again, I encourage you to find and follow a model as a way to induct yourself into this work.

The Active Engagement

Almost always, the active engagement will be a time when children try the strategy that you have just taught, and they do so by writing-in-the-air (talking as if they are writing) to a partner. For example, if you have taught that toward the end of their work on a text, writers reread their own writing to ask, "Does this make sense?" then you'll want to use the active engagement time as a chance to provide children with some scaffolded practice doing this. You have two common options. One option is for you to say, "So, right now, while you sit in front of me, would you get out your own writing and read just the first paragraph as if you are a stranger, asking yourself, 'Does this make sense?' If you spot a place where it is confusing, put a question mark in the margin." The advantage of asking children to try the strategy this way is that you help children apply the minilesson to their own work and help them get started at it. The disadvantage is that sometimes kids can't use the teaching point of the day on just any paragraph (as they could in this example), and therefore it is not possible for them to find a place in their current piece where the strategy applies and put the strategy into operation

all within just a few short minutes. This portion of a minilesson shouldn't take more than four minutes! Then, too, you can't provide much scaffolding or do much teaching off this work because each child will be working with a different piece of writing.

You might, therefore, say, "Would you help me with my piece by becoming a reader of my next paragraph? Would Partner 1 read it quietly aloud and, as you read, think, 'Does this make sense?' Partner 2, you listen and give your partner a thumbs up if yes, you think it is making sense." By using your writing for the active engagement, you have a common text to discuss if problems arise in applying the strategy. Also, when children have applied the strategy to your writing, they can also transfer the strategy to their own writing once the minilesson is over and they are on their own. Otherwise, the teaching of the minilesson won't carry into the workshop time and may be less likely to carry into each child's writing life.

Sometimes the active engagement portion of the minilesson does not involve partner work; each child works individually, often guided by the teacher's nudges. Teachers listen in on what children do, sometimes intervening to lift the level of a particular child's work. You will often end the time by reporting back on the good work one child did.

The Link

During the link portion of the minilesson, you will usually repeat the teaching point verbatim, adding it to a chart as you do so. You won't have one amalgamated chart that lists every teaching point that has ever been taught! Each chart will feature a collection of strategies writers can use to accomplish a particular goal. That is, the title of the chart generally names the goal, and then below this there will be a growing list of strategies writers might draw upon to accomplish that goal. Charts lose their effectiveness if they are too long. Typically, charts do not contain more than five or six specific items.

Generally, the link is a time for you to tell children when to use what you have taught them. You will be apt to say something like, "When you are [in this situation as a writer] and you want to [achieve this goal], then you might use any one of these strategies," and you reread your charted list. "Another option would be to use this strategy," and you add the new strategy to the list. Usually, in the link, you will say something like, "So today, you have lots of choices. You can do this, or that, or this, or that."

PLAN CONFERENCES, ASSESSMENTS, HOMEWORK, AND THE REST

Planning a unit can't be equated to just writing minilessons! First of all, once you have planned a sequence of minilessons, you can read through them, imagining the challenges they will pose for your children. You'll be able to ascertain that for some minilessons, many of your children will need extra support, and those will be good places to plan small-group strategy lessons. You may decide that on some of those occasions, you will go from table to table, providing close-in demonstrations of whatever it is you hope children will do first, then circling back for demonstrations of whatever you hope children will do next. For these extra-challenging minilessons, you will probably want to plan follow-up minilessons, devising those after you study the particular ways your children are encountering difficulty.

Then, too, you'll want to plan how you will assess children's progress. You might think that the time to assess is at the end of a unit, but in fact, it is wise to mark several whole-class checkpoints within the unit as well, to tailor your teaching accordingly. One way to do this is to plan to use the checklists and rubrics we have included within this series. You might use them on your own (or with colleagues) after school, sorting students' writing in piles according to where it mostly falls along the learning progressions we've provided. Or you might want to recruit students to join you in assessing their progress—setting them up with their ongoing work and the checklists most appropriate to their development and kind of writing, asking them to see for themselves where they are strong and where they can aim to grow. You might also look back at their work at the beginning of the unit to see what teaching seems to have taken hold since then. In a narrative unit, are they writing about focused events, organizing their narratives chronologically, and storytelling rather than summarizing? In an essay unit, are they gathering entries that contain possible thesis statements? If not, you'll need to plan and devise new sessions accordingly, so you will leave some time and space for sessions you'll create as a result of these assessments.

You can plan for any other aspect of your teaching as well. For example, you could plan how partnerships might be tweaked so that they support the goals of the unit. You might think about particular language lessons that English language learners may need in a unit. You will also want to plan the at-home work you expect students to do during a unit. This will be especially important for any units that require research. Often the only way to keep the pace of the unit going is to assign research-based homework so that the main work students are doing in workshop is the writing itself!

Because your units of study will be written down, you and your colleagues can put them on the table and think together about these plans. "What's good here that we can add onto?" you can ask. "What's not so good that we can fix?" And that yearly improvement, of course, is the goal for all of our teaching—these units we've crafted as well as the ones you'll invent on your own with your colleagues.